Productivity Based Management

Studies in Productivity Analysis

Ali Dogramaci, Editor
Rutgers University

Titles in the Series:
Adam, Dogramaci, Productivity Analysis at the Organizational Level
Dogramaci, Adam; Aggregate and Industry-Level Productivity Analysis
Dogramaci; Productivity Analysis: A Range of Perspectives
Dogramaci; Developments in Econometric Analyses of Productivity: Measurement and Modelling Issues

Productivity Based Management

Ephraim F. Sudit

Rutgers, The State University of New Jersey

SPRINGER SCIENCE+BUSINESS MEDIA, B.V.

Distributors for North America:
Kluwer Academic Publishers, Boston
190 Old Derby Street
Hingham, MA 02043, U.S.A.

Distributors Outside North America:
Kluwer Academic Publishers Group
Distribution Centre
P. O. Box 322
3300AH Dordrecht, The Netherlands

Library of Congress Cataloging in Publication Data

Sudit, Ephraim F.
Productivity based management.

(Studies in productivity analysis)
Bibliography: p.
1. Industrial productivity. 2. Industrial management.
I. Title.
HD56.S83 1984 658.5 83-20001
ISBN 978-94-011-9669-7 ISBN 978-94-011-9667-3 (eBook)
DOI 10.1007/978-94-011-9667-3

Softcover reprint of the hardcover 1st edition 1984

Dedicated to My Wife and My Mother

PREFACE

Realization of productivity gains is a necessary condition for long-term consistent improvement in economic well being. We have to work smarter and produce more efficiently to attain an ever higher quantity and quality of goods and services without sacrificing leisure. This is true for the economy at large as well as for individual firms. In a competitive environment, businesses must continuously improve the productivity of their operations in order to sustain and augment profitability and growth. This basic requirement may be temporarily obscured by unexpected external developments or financial manipulations, but it is nevertheless essential to the long-term health of any economic enterprise. Increasing awareness of the importance of productivity has recently motivated renewed interest in the development and refinement of productivity-based management techniques. The purpose of this book is to review and evaluate some of the new contributions in this area.

The analysis of productivity-based management in this book encompasses planning, decision making and control methods which explicitly incorporate techniques designed to measure, monitor, induce and improve underlying productivity performance in production, financial planning, marketing and international operations. These productivity-based methods can easily accommodate built-in efficiency incentives designed to motivate people working in decentralized organizations toward goal congruent behavior. It is argued throughout the book that productivity-based management, at its best, is likely to improve significantly the efficiency and effectiveness of economic enterprises. In fact, many of the productivity-based methods described in this book have been successfully implemented in recent years in a variety of managerial settings.

This book is intended primarily for general managers, professional analysts and students of management in the private and public sectors. The predominant emphasis is on applied analysis and practical managerial applications. Only very basic quantitative skills are necessary to follow the discussion. At the same time, I did not try to cover all or even most areas of applied productivity analysis. Instead, I have selected an array of methods and approaches which, in my view, appear to be among the promising tools for the enhancement of effective management.

Many of the ideas in this book are based on joint published research with my colleagues at Rutgers University, New York University, Columbia University, The University of Haifa and the American Telephone and Telegraph Company. In writing this book, I have therefore greatly benefited from my work with Ali Chaudry, Michael Crew, Dan Eldor, Harsharanjeet S. Jagpal, Akira Ishikawa, Paul Kleindorfer, Abraham Ravid, Melvin Shakun and H.D. Vinod. For very helpful advice and assistance in planning this work I owe a debt of gratitude to Ali Dogramaci. I would also like to thank Lorraine Kenny for her most competent typing and technical assistance. Finally, I am most grateful to my wife Myriam Sudit for her professional and editorial assistance, as well as for her patience and encouragement.

CONTENTS

Productivity Based Management

1 THE PRODUCTIVITY CONCEPT: DEFINITION, MEASUREMENT AND MANAGERIAL IMPORTANCE

Alternative Productivity Measures

Productivity is probably one of the most common, and at the same time one of the vaguest concepts in the linguistics of Business and Management. Like the concept of quality, we think we know it intuitively, yet we soon discover that numerous difficulties are inherent in the precise conceptual definition of productivity, let alone its empirical measurement. The objective of this chapter is to review the relative merits of some of the most widely used measures of total factor productivity.

The term "productivity" is usually operationalized in terms of ratios of outputs to inputs, defined in physical terms or the equivalent. The productivity analysis is intended to shed light upon the efficiency of the production process in the firm. To this end, *quantities* of outputs and inputs (e.g., volumes of goods or services for outputs, manhours for labor inputs, and machine hours for capital inputs) for proxies thereof are measured rather than their nominal monetary values.

Productivity analysis of a purposeful productive system comprised of more than one distinct activity usually envisions the production process as a "black box"—inputs flowing in, outputs flowing out. It concentrates on levels and variations in input-output relationships to gain some insights about the overall efficiency of this production process. Tasks of a management oriented productivity analysis thus include the proper specification and measurement of output-input ratios, the identification of some of the basic factors affecting these productivity variations, and the assessment of their relative contribution to productivity performance.

The ratio of an aggregate of outputs to an aggregate of inputs is commonly known as the Total Factor Productivity (TFP) index. By contrast, partial productivity indexes are ratios of aggregate output to some inputs only. For example, the frequently used output per manhour or labor productivity index is a partial productivity measure. The main reason for its wide use is a practical one—nonavailability of good data on inputs of capital that are needed for the computation of a total factor productivity index.

We generally think of total factor productivity as an overall measure of productive efficiency in the use of resources. If the same physical volume of total inputs can produce a larger physical volume of output, we tend to interpret this as increased productive efficiency. The same cannot be readily deduced from changes in partial productivity indexes because variations in these ratios can result merely from changes in the combinations of inputs, with no change either in overall efficiency or in the efficiencies of the particular inputs.

For the sake of simplicity let us consider companies that employ only two factors of production: capital and labor. For such companies, increases in output per manhour and total factor productivity will be numerically identical as long as the capital-labor ratio remains unchanged. Thus, if these enterprises experience stable ratios of capital to labor over time, increases in their output per manhour will constitute a good numerical approximation of their increases in total factor productivity. On the other hand, for companies whose technological advances are accompanied by heavy capital investment relative to growth in labor input, the increases in output per manhour will exceed the increases in total factor productivity. Thus, the reason "labor productivity" should be interpreted cautiously when used to describe output per manhour for an individual company or industry is that a significant portion of the increase in output per manhour may be often attributable to the substitution of capital for labor (i.e., labor having more and better capital to work with). It is therefore erroneous to equate, in general, changes in the ratio of output to one input with the productivity performance or contribution of that particular input. Total factor productivity gains can be shown to be a weighted sum of partial productivity gains. For example, if three inputs were involved in production—labor, capital and materials, then the total factor productivity gain can be represented as a weighted sum of the changes in output per manhour, output per unit of capital and output per unit of materials. Nonetheless, the share of each input component in the weighted TFP gain does not necessarily reflect the contribution of the productivity of that input to total productivity.

The total factor productivity gain can be viewed as a change in aggregate output that is not accounted for by changes in inputs. The underlying rationale of this view is that in the absence of any productivity gains a given proportional change in all the inputs, with their composition unchanged, will result in the same proportional increase in output. Productivity changes, then, are seen as occurring whenever the output does not increase in the same proportion as the inputs. Advances (declines) in productivity are registered when rates of growth in output exceed (fall short of) the rates of growth in all inputs.

This type of productivity change can be attributed to the effects of all factors operating on the productive process, other than mere changes in the quantities of inputs. These other factors may include changes in technology, economies of scale, changes in operating methods, utilization rates, managerial efficiency, and so on. Because of the multiplicity of the factors involved, and the difficulty of tracing their specific contributions to productivity growth, we must resort to this overall measure of productivity, which essentially represents an unexplained residual. For this reason, the TFP residual is sometimes termed "a measure of our ignorance" with regard to the unknown or intangible factors affecting output. It is particularly noteworthy that conventional TFP measures incorporate changes in efficiency associated with scale. Consequently changes in levels of output will usually affect productivity, and one should not assume that a certain observed TFP performance is feasible at any level of output.

Aggregation Problems

So far, we have discussed total factor productivity in terms of the relationships between aggregate inputs and aggregate outputs, entirely bypassing the problem as to how individual inputs and outputs are aggregated. Quantities of inputs and outputs are measured in different and diverse units. Simple addition of manhours and machine-hours, or for that matter, manhours of different occupational categories, would be equivalent to adding apples and oranges. Consequently, the problems associated with the aggregation of all physical inputs to a total input index, and the aggregation of all outputs to a total output index are quite complex and constitute one of the core dilemmas in the construction of total factor productivity indexes. In technical language, it is said that aggregator input and output functions using appropriate aggregation rules have to be specified. In simple English, it means that appropriate weights must be applied to individual inputs and outputs in order to properly derive total inputs and total outputs.

Consider a production system completely defined by an implicit multi-input multi-output production function F:

$$F(\bar{Y}, \bar{X}) = 0, \tag{1.1}$$

where $\bar{Y} = (Y_1, Y_2, \ldots, Y_m)$, $\bar{X} = (X_1, X_2, \ldots, X_n)$. $\bar{X}$ and $\bar{Y}$ are respectively n-component real input and m-component real output vectors. F represents the technological state of the art. Inputs in production and productivity analysis represent a physical rather than monetary flow of services, for example man hours for labor and machine hours for capital.

In a world of complete certainty and perfect knowledge, it would be possible to identify all tangible and intangible inputs and outputs and to specify their precise interrelationship, F. Consequently, our TFP ignorance residual would be reduced to zero, thereby reducing the importance of conventional input-output indexes as measures of productivity. Productivity measures thus serve as useful indicators of levels and changes in productive efficiency when some of the inputs and outputs are unknown or unmeasurable (i.e., $\bar{Y}$, $\bar{X}$ and F are incompletely specified).

The basic assumption behind most theoretical and applied productivity analyses is the separability assumption, which stipulates that all efficient production possibilities can be represented by an equality between aggregate levels of inputs and outputs obtained by their respective *separate* underlying aggregator functions g and f. Mathematically, this assumption allows the specification of (1.1) as:

$$g(\bar{Y}) = f(\bar{X}). \tag{1.2}$$

The separability assumption is economically restrictive since most production processes, do *not* in general exhibit *independence* of efficient input and output substitution possibilities. In a complex technology, changes in the input-possibilities functions are likely to affect output-possibilities functions. Nonetheless most productivity measurements resort to diverse versions of the separability assumption since it greatly facilitates the specification and estimation of multi-input single-output or multi-input multi-output production functions or productivity indexes.

If components of an aggregate which vary equi-proportionately are simply added, the variation in the aggregate will not be biased. In most dynamic production processes, the equi-proportionate assumption rarely holds. Technical change, for example, is often characterized by increasing capital intensity brought about by almost continuous substitution of labor inputs for capital inputs over time. Consequently, if, as is often the case, we use in productivity analysis improperly aggregated data (i.e., input or output components that were added together without using explicit weights), then possible biases in input and output aggregates may result. As shown by Star (1974), proper disaggregation will decrease (increase) TFP when the input with the highest (lowest) price or share grows the fastest. Thus productivity studies using improperly aggregated inputs and outputs are likely to produce aggregation-biased TFP estimates. On the input side, if occurrence of technical change manifests itself in increasing prices of certain technically related inputs, productivity measurement based on improper aggregation may overestimate TFP. Indeed, Star (1974) shows this to be precisely the case for residual estimates for the U.S. economy for the 1950–1960 period. Disaggregation of capital into equipment and structures and disaggregation of labor by sex, occupation, age, education, and race reduced the growth of the residual TFP as a percentage of annual growth in value added from 48 percent to 27 percent. Moreover, changing the order of disaggregation of labor affects the magnitude of changes in the residual's role in growth. Problems of the same nature are likely to occur in TFP measurement of industries, firms and segments of companies. In practice, these aggregation problems can rarely be attenuated without resorting to considerably more complex and costly methods of productivity analysis.

Total Factor Productivity Indexes

Numerous "early generation" productivity studies (e.g., Abramovitz, 1956; Fabricant, 1942; Denison, 1962, 1974; Kendrick, 1961, 1973) used modified Laspeyres or Paasche TFP indexes. Factor (input) prices were assigned as weights to the respective inputs to obtain total factor input aggregates. These factor price weights were fixed relative to a preselected base year level. The input aggregator functions underlying these TFP measures are thus linearly homogeneous additive production functions. As observed by Nadiri (1970), a constant return-to-scale, constant elasticity of substitution (CES) production function is consistent with Kendrick's underlying total factor input function. Common to most of these productivity studies is the use of a readily available single output measure (e.g., GNP in constant base year prices), without any explicit treatment of or reference to the underlying problems of the aggregation of the component outputs. The resulting TFP measures were thus asymmetric and subject to possible aggregation bias. However, Laspeyres and Paasche indexes can be also applied to multi-output production processes by assigning fixed "base" year output prices as weights to their respective output quantities. These fixed weight indexes can be modified by changing those weights every few years through the selection of a more recent reference period for input and output prices.

Modified Laspeyres, Paasche, or geometric indexes of the type referred to above suffer from inherent index number biases, either overestimating or underestimating changes in TFP aggregates. Also, such input quantity indexes do not conform to Fisher's (1922) reversal rule (i.e., the product of the factor price and the quantity indexes should yield the total cost ratio between any two periods) which is a desirable property for appropriate separation of price and quantity effects. To correct for these index measurement deficiencies, "second generation" productivity studies (e.g., Solow, 1957; Jorgenson and Griliches, 1967; Christensen and Jorgenson, 1970; Hulten, 1975, 1979; Star, 1974) usually use Divisia (1926) input and output indexes. Solow (1957) was among the first to show that Divisia TFP index forms can be naturally derived from simple production relationships.

Divisia indexes have a number of attractive properties. They can be shown to be unbiased subject to certain assumptions regarding underlying production, thereby eliminating index-number biases related to base-year choices. Divisia indexes also exhibit the reproductive property. A discrete Divisia index of discrete Divisia indexes is a discrete Divisia index of the components. The latter property is particularly important for productivity analysis of whole enterprises where aggregate variables are obtained by means of aggregation of subaggregates. Finally, Divisia indexes conform to Fisher's reversal rule.

The derivation of continuous Divisia indexes is relatively simple. Assuming competitive markets for all outputs and all factors of production (including capital), we obtain the following equation of total revenues and total costs plus normal profits:

$$\sum_{j=1}^{m} P_j Y_j = \sum_{i=1}^{n} W_i X_i, \tag{1.3}$$

where P_j and W_i are the unit prices of the jth output and the ith input, respectively. Normal profits are represented by the products of the competitive cost of capital and the quantities of the capital inputs.

Totally differentiating (1.3) with respect to time, we obtain

$$\sum_{j=1}^{m} \dot{P}_j Y_j + \sum_{j=1}^{m} P_j \dot{Y}_j = \sum_{i=1}^{n} \dot{W}_i X_i + \sum_{i=1}^{n} W_i \dot{X}_i, \tag{1.4}$$

where $\cdot$ denotes differentiation with respect to time. Dividing and multiplying each term in (1.4) by the base-level value of its respective changing variable, and then dividing the right-hand and left-hand sides of equation (1.3) by $\Sigma_{i=1}^{n} = W_iX_i$ and $\Sigma_{j=1}^{m} = P_jY_j$, respectively, and rearranging, we get:

$$\sum_{j=1}^{m} \frac{\dot{Y}_j}{Y_j} \beta_j - \sum_{i=1}^{n} \frac{\dot{X}_i}{X_i} \alpha_i = \sum_{i=1}^{n} \frac{\dot{W}_i}{W_i} \alpha_i - \sum_{j=1}^{m} \frac{\dot{P}_j}{P_j} \beta_j, \tag{1.5}$$

where:

$$\alpha_i = \frac{W_iX_i}{\sum_{i=1}^{n} W_iX_i}$$

is the share of the cost of the i-th input in total factor cost and

$$\beta_j = \frac{P_jY_j}{\sum_{j=1}^{m} P_jY_j}$$

is the share of the revenue of the j-th output in total revenues.

The left-hand expression in (1.5)—the difference between the sums of the weighted changes in the quantities of outputs and inputs—is, by definition, the continuous expression for the percentage change in the TFP Divisia index. The expression in (1.5) reflects the duality between changes in quantities and unit prices. Thus, the percentage changes in TFP could be expressed as the differences in the sums of percentage changes in weighted unit input prices and output prices. Rearrangement of (1.5) reveals that Divisia indexes conform with Fisher's reversal rule.

Note however, that the validity of (1.5) depends on the existence of competitive input and output markets. In noncompetitive markets prices and quantities will not be independent of each other. The differentiation of (1.3) with respect to time will be therefore more complex and require knowledge of demand patterns for outputs and factors of production. Thus, for enterprises operating in noncompetitive output or input markets conventional TFP measures are likely to be biased.

Unbiased and Unique Discrete Approximations to TFP Indexes

The expressions for changes in TFP Divisia indexes derived in (1.5) are based on continuous infinitesimal changes over time. Empirically, time series of cross-sectional economic data are available at discrete intervals. Thus, the choice and use of unbiased and unique discrete approximations to continuous forms constitute a problem of no small importance in productivity.

Laspeyres or Paasche indexes are formulated in discrete terms. As pointed out earlier, it can be shown that they are likely to produce biased approximations to their underlying continuous additive aggregator functions. As for the Divisia TFP index, if we denote its path over the time interval $(0,T)$ as $\gamma(t)$, then, following (1.5), we can express its continuous form over $(0,T)$, TFP $(0,T)$ as

$$\text{TFP}(0,T) = \exp\left\{\phi_0^T \mid \sum_j \frac{\dot{Y}_j(t)}{Y_j(t)}\, \beta_j(t) - \sum_i \frac{\dot{X}_i(t)}{X_i(t)}\alpha_i(t) \mid d\gamma(t)\right\} \qquad (1.6)$$

The Divisia index TFP $(0,T)$ thus represents a set of paths (t) over the time interval $(0,T)$. Being a line integral, it is path-dependent, which gives rise to the problem of cycling (i.e., indicating *a range of values* for the same input-output technical changes).

The guarantee uniqueness (i.e., the absence of cycling), TFP $(0,T)$ has to be path-independent. Hulten (1973) has shown that the necessary and sufficient conditions for path independence are as follows:

1. The existence of total factor input and total factor output aggregates;
2. Linear homogeneity of the aggregates in condition 1 above;
3. The existence of normalized value shares, α_i's and β_j's for aggregate components that are observable and unique up to a scalar multiplication.

Of the above conditions, the first merely requires that true values be associated with the aggregate components of the TFP index. For a single output case, condition 2 reduces to a constant returns-to-scale requirement. Condition 3 seems to require some sort of optimal behavior (e.g., profit maximization) on the part of production agents. Otherwise, the uniqueness of the α_i's and β_j's cannot be guaranteed. What this amounts to in practical terms is that a Divisia TFP index is likely to be a biased measure of technical change to the extent that the firm in question deviates from optimal behavior constant returns to scale in production, faces noncompetitive markets, and inappropriately aggregates inputs and outputs.

Following Törnqvist (1936) and Theil (1968), the discrete counterpart of (1.5) is generally recommended for TFP Divisia indexes as follows:

$$\frac{\mathrm{TFP}_{t+1}}{\mathrm{TFP}_t} = \frac{\prod_{j=1}^{m} \left(\frac{Y_{j,t+1}}{Y_{j,t}} \right)^{1/2(\beta_{j,t}+\beta_{j,t+1})}}{\prod_{i=1}^{n} \left(\frac{X_{i,t+1}}{X_{i,t}} \right)^{1/2(\alpha_{i,t}+\alpha_{i,t+1})}} \tag{1.7}$$

Diewert (1976) has shown that the Törnqvist TFP quantity index in (1.7) is exact for a linearly homogeneous translog aggregator function. This is an attractive property since a linearly homogeneous translog function has been shown by Christensen, Jorgenson, and Lau (1973) to be a second-order local approximation to an arbitrary twice-continuous differentiable linear homogeneous function. Consequently, researchers using Divisia TFP indexes cannot be accused, within the limits of second-order approximation, of arbitrarily prechoosing restrictive underlying production structures. This explains in part the extensive use of Divisia indexes in recent productivity research (see Christensen and Jorgenson, 1970; Star, 1974; Hulten, 1979).

Value Added Versus Gross Output

For an economy, real value added is defined as the aggregate volume of all final goods and services net of all intermediate goods. A traditionally defined national product adjusted for price changes usually serves as a proxy for such real value added. For industries or companies, the price-adjusted value of goods and services purchased from outside the system are subtracted from gross output (total revenues in constant dollars) to obtain real value added. The relationship of real value added to the production function inclusive of all inputs is at best ambiguous. Since real value added (VA) is defined as the difference between separately deflated gross output (Y) and intermediate inputs (M), the use of value added in aggregate productivity studies as a measure of output implicitly assumes that the underlying production function is additive-separable of the form $Y = VA + M$. Consequently, while the use of a deflated value-added measure of output in macro-economic productivity analysis is convenient from the point of view of macro-data availability, Bruno (1978) and Diewert (1978) showed that it is valid only under very restrictive assumptions with regard to production technology or in cases where prices of outputs and intermediate inputs vary in strict proportion. This conclusion is even more directly applicable to measurement of TFP of individual companies. Apart from their restrictiveness, value-added productivity measures, by excluding intermediate materials from both input and output aggregates, fail to capture their full impact on productivity. For example, value-added-based TFP measures may, to a degree, distort changes in productivity advances related to substitution of labor for energy and energy-intensive capital.

As a result of these difficulties, gross output measures rather than value-added measures should be used for company and industry studies. These measures, by including intermediate goods purchased from outside, capture the impact of make-buy decisions on the total productivity of the firm. On the company level, such data are usually readily available. On the industry level, data facilitating separation between intermediate materials purchased within the industry and intermediate goods purchased from outside the industry have to be secured for gross output productivity analysis. On the economy level, for the purposes of assessing productivity of the national production network, a gross output measure inclusive of all intermediate commodities may be preferable. If the national economic welfare implications of productivity changes are to be analyzed, a resort to value-added TFP indexes for macro-economic analyses only may be necessary in spite of their restrictiveness.

The Concept and Measurement of Capital

Few areas in economics are as unsettled and controversial as the question of the appropriate conceptualization, definition, and measurement of capital. Since capital is a major primary input in classical and neo-classical production theory and productivity analysis, these issues are of major importance to our discussion.

Capital stock is usually conceptualized as a stock of produced (man-made) tools of production (e.g., a stock of x machines.) This stock renders a flow of services (inputs) to the production process (e.g., machine hours.) In the context of the economic system as a whole, the capital input is an intermediate commodity. This realization raises serious problems with regard to the appropriate interpretation of the relationship between levels of capital inputs and their contributions to outputs. As summarized by Robinson (1969, p. 310), "Looking at the matter in a philosophical light, the reason why there is no meaning to be attached to the marginal product of 'capital' is that, from a long-run point of view, labor and natural resources are the factors of production in the economy as a whole, while capital goods and the time patterns of production are the means by which the factors are deployed."

The fact that capital is an intermediate product raises questions as to whether Solow's (1957) separation between movement along a production function reflecting scale effects and shifts of the production function (reflecting productivity or technical change) is meaningful in a dynamic production environment. Along the lines argued by Rymes (1971) and Malinvaud (1953), capital accumulation (investment) can be viewed as an intermediate good including technical change and thereby facilitating consumption growth.

These considerations led Hulten (1979) to propose a dynamic measure of TFP change inclusive of the productivity-induced accumulation of capital, which he terms the *dynamic residual*. This dynamic residual, in contrast to the conventional residual described above, allows for the effects of capital accumulation by treating investment as an intermediate good and consumption as the only direct delivery of final demand. By contrast, the conventional residual may significantly understate the portion of growth attributable to technical change by failing to account for the reproducibility of capital and its productivity-inducing effect.

It is noteworthy that in a long term macro-economic context, a conceptualization of capital as an intermediate commodity leads to a significant change in our definition of macro-economic output. In this context, the volume of consumption goods represents the only direct delivery of final demand to be qualified as output. Investment, a component in the traditional value-added measure of output, should by this logic be excluded on the grounds that it should be treated similarly to other intermediate materials not counted among the final commodities of which GNP components are comprised.

Traditional productivity analyses on the macro level as well as on the firm level inevitably resort to some notion of an aggregate capital input. However, the very existence and meaning of the concept of aggregate capital are debatable, being subject to one of the most acrimonious controversies in the history of the economic profession. In the first place, it seems exceedingly difficult, if not impossible, to define an aggregate capital entity measured in constant dollars that is independent of the price of capital. The absence of such independence leads to circuitous reasoning that derives marginalist conditions for equilibria interest rates in capital markets as functions of capital inputs and at the same time views prices of capital commodities as determined in part by interest rate-discounting incorporated in their expected present-value estimation. This interdependence between capital prices and traditional dollar denominated proxies for capital quantity measures is also associated with switching phenomena of multiple, input-price-dependent, cost-efficient capital-inputs levels for the same technologies. Pasinetti (1977) offers an excellent review of these issues that questions the existence of the traditional neoclassical aggregate production function as visualized by Solow (1957). Hulten (1979), in his development and estimation of the dynamic residual, addresses these problems only partially. Ultimately, for the purposes of long-term "black box"-type of macro-productivity analysis only, it may be advantageous to think of consumption volume as output and labor and natural resources as primary inputs. A more detailed analysis of the process and phases of aggregate production may have to draw upon Sraffa's (1960) analytical framework of production of commodities by means of commodities.

For productivity analysis of individual companies some of these capital measurement problems are less acute. For a single economic enterprise capital inputs can usually be considered as primary inputs rather than intermediate inputs. With the exception of vertically integrated firms the output of individual companies consists of products and services designed for consumers or other companies regardless of whether they are consumption or investment goods. Thus most firms can justifiably treat capital as a primary input and need not concern themselves with the separation between consumption output and investment output. However, the problems associated with the interdependence between real dollar measures of capital stocks and the cost of capital remain largely unresolved.

Apart from the conceptual difficulties, measurement problems of aggregate capital inputs abound. There is currently, however, a degree of consensus among applied researchers that (1) disaggregation to types of plant, equipment, and tools is desirable; (2) imputation of flows of capital services rather than stocks of capital should be used so as to treat all inputs and outputs as flows of goods and services: and (3) capital inputs should be adjusted for degree of utilization and depreciation whenever the data are available. There is less agreement as to how to reprice different vintages, handle intertemporal effects of capital on output, and separate changes in quantities of capital services from changes in quality and embodied technologies for the purposes of construction of aggregate TFP indexes.

It should be emphasized that estimation of capital services inevitably requires imputation of nonmarket transactions. In view of the conceptual and measurement difficulties involved, variations and error margins in capital input estimations may be very large. These differences are in turn likely to have a very significant effect on TFP results. The reader could compare differences in TFP results obtained from the same underlying macro–

economic data by Christensen and Jorgenson (1970) and Hulten (1979) and study the differences between Denison (1962) and Jorgenson and Griliches (1967), who utilize different capital measurement techniques for the same data. Significant TFP differences of similar magnitudes could emerge when such different capital measurement methods are applied to productivity analyses on the firm level.

Productivity Measures and Financial Statements

Although productivity measures draw on financial statements they do not use accounting data directly. Productivity measures are designed to reflect "physical" gains or losses. Outputs and inputs are measured in physical units or in money measures adjusted for price changes to approximate changes in physical units. Thus, while profit measures reflect both physical and monetary factors, productivity measures single out physical flows only. In addition, productivity measures are constructed within the framework of economic analysis, and while making full use of accounting data, they are not bound by such accounting rules as the valuation of assets at historical cost or application of conventional depreciation rates. It follows, therefore, that changes in profits and productivity are not necessarily correlated for any and all periods, although in most enterprises a positive association between *long-term* productivity gains and increases in profits should normally be expected.

Figure 1-1 highlights the basic relationship between accounting data and TFP indexes. Revenues or sales in income statements are products of prices and quantities which relate to goods and services *sold*. Total output in a TFP index is a weighted aggregate of quantities of goods and services *produced.* These quantities are measured directly in terms of physical units produced. Alternatively, they can be indirectly estimated by adjusting (deflating) the revenue generated by each product for changes in its own price levels. The resulting revenues stated in constant prices may be interpreted as proxies of real volumes. If deflated revenues are used as indicators of output then appropriate inventory adjustments must be undertaken to reconcile the transition from revenues which are based on units of output sold to units of physical output produced.

Labor inputs are measured by person hours worked for each distinct occupational category. Simple addition of person hours of different labor skills and occupations is tantamount to adding apples and oranges. To avoid aggregation biases of this type each category of person hours can be weighted by its respective employment compensation per person hours. Differentials

COMPONENTS OF FINANCIAL STATEMENTS	COMPONENTS OF TFP
REVENUES (SALES) Sum of quantities *sold* multiplied by their respective prices	TOTAL OUTPUT Aggregate of Quantities of goods and services *produced* weighted by their respective revenue shares
TOTAL LABOR COMPENSATION EXPENSES Sum of salaries and fringe benefits paid to all Employees	LABOR INPUTS Aggregate of hours worked for different occupational categories weighted by their respective shares in total labor compensation
MATERIALS RENTS AND SERVICES EXPENSES Costs of all materials rents and services purchased from outsiders	MATERIALS RENTS AND SERVICES INPUTS Weighted aggregates of quantities of materials used and real (deflated) values of rents and services
CAPITAL RELATED EXPENSES Depreciation Expenses Interest Expenses FIXED ASSETS (BOOK VALUES) Plant and Equipment Buildings Land	CAPITAL INPUTS Aggregate of quantity of different types of machine-hours weighted by their respective cost shares Real (deflated) value of buildings and rent multiplied by the cost of capital

Figure 1-1. Accounting Data and Total Factor Productivity Measurement

in compensation rates of firms operating in competitive labor markets are presumed to reflect, at least partially, differences in quality and contribution to output of diverse types of labor. Applying these weights, we can obtain an aggregate of person hours worked to represent total labor input.

Inputs of materials, rents and services represent factors of production purchased by the firm from outside producers and suppliers. Materials are measured by physical units and weighted in aggregation by their respective prices. Physical quantities or volumes of rents and services are usually difficult to measure directly. Consequently, nominal dollar values of rents and services are deflated by their respective price indices and the computed real dollar values serve as proxies for quantities.

Capital inputs are usually the most difficult to measure since they involve nonmarket transactions. Capital assets such as plant, equipment, machinery, building and land are owned by the firm and provide services to the firm. The quantities of these services can be measured by machine hours, tool hours, building hours and land hours. The value of these services, in the absence of market transactions, can be only inputed. The opportunity costs of tying up the necessary funds to own these assets, as reflected by their ongoing market value, divided by the hours of production services that they provide, give us approximations of cost per hour of capital service. Weighting these hours of services provided by the different capital assets by their respective costs per hours furnishes us with weighted aggregates of capital inputs. It is thus possible to estimate the physical flow of productive services, measured in capital asset hours, which are generated by each particular capital asset owned by the firm, as well as to impute the capital cost of each asset hour. Since fixed assets are stated in the balance sheet at book value, imputation of costs of capital require estimation of their market value. Economic depreciation expenses are reflected in appreciation or depreciation of market values and interest expenses are reflected in the estimation of the opportunity cost of capital for the firm. Thus, all accounting entries related to capital (fixed asset values, depreciation charges and interest expenses) must be restated to provide the best possible estimates of economic realities.

If Divisia methods are used to compute total factor productivity, then their physical input and outputs are weighted by the respective shares of their own revenues or costs in total revenues or costs in accordance with (1.7). If Laspeyres' indexes are used, then inputs and outputs are weighted by base year prices to render productivity indexes of the type:

$$\mathrm{TFP}_t = \frac{\Sigma_j P_{oj} Y_{tj}}{\Sigma_i W_{oi} X_{ti}} \tag{1.8}$$

where P_{oj} is the price of the j-th output at $t = o$ and W_{oi} is the price the i-th input at $t = 0$.

Accounting and economic measures of profitability are designed as indicators of the financial health of the firm. Productivity measures serve as indicators of the physical health of the firm. In the short term, favorable profitability performance due to temporary external factors may obscure deterioration in efficiency or productivity performance. Alternatively, temporary weak profits may obscure internal productivity strength, thereby inhibiting appropriate planning for exploiting future opportunities. Consequently, profitability indicators and other financial ratios stated in nominal terms only often provide inadequate or potentially misleading information for managerial decision making. Hence, financial statement data need to be supplemented by productivity data to provide for a more comprehensive and useful management information base.

Objectives and Uses of Productivity Indexes

The primary objective of total factor productivity indexes is to provide measures of levels and trends of overall productive efficiency in the utilization of given resources. An increase in productivity means that the company can produce the same level of output with a lesser quantity of resources or a greater amount of output with the same resources. Whatever the reasons for such variations in productive efficiency, their measurement is important for the following reasons:

1. Computations of total factor productivity figures over time point to levels and trends in the productive efficiency of the company. Productivity gains are normally a significant source of increased benefits to stockholders, employees, and customers. Productivity trends have thus a direct bearing on the most important aspects of company performance, such as its rate of return to stockholders, the quality and morale of its human organization, customer loyalty, etc. Productivity variations may provide clues to some of the reasons behind the improvement or deterioration in key aspects of company performance.
2. Measures of total factor productivity over time may be used for comparison with similar measures in *related* industries, to give a relative measure of productive efficiency. Such comparisons with other enterprises exposed to similar external economic conditions, if done with proper caution, may provide bases for setting competitive goals or

improving business performance. This can also be done for operating units of the same enterprise.

3. Past productivity figures may be used as bases for long term and short term forecasting of future trends. These forecasts can provide information relating to such important questions as (a) the extent to which productivity gains might offset rising costs and permit a flexible pricing policy, or (b) the labor and capital resources that would be needed to produce a given volume of output. Reliable productivity forecasts can therefore play an important role in long term corporate planning, capital budgeting, as well as in short term financial planning and operational budgeting.
4. A comprehensive productivity data base opens new important avenues of research into factors affecting productivity and the formulation and estimation of production and cost functions, which can contribute to our understanding of the basic economic characteristics underlying the financial performance of the business.
5. Productivity measures can have important managerial uses in the public and regulated sectors in evaluating efficiency levels in government operations and improving pricing decisions in government enterprises and regulated companies.

In conclusion, TFP analysis is aimed at the identification, measurement, and analysis of the unexplained residual, or the magnitude of our ignorance about the production process. This is indeed a useful pursuit if we accept the Socratic view that knowing how much we do not know is the beginning of all knowledge. More often than not, this type of analysis takes us to the limits of available information. At the very least, measurement and analysis of the TFP residual should be helpful in (1) identifying the portions of output growth that cannot be explained by changes in tangible inputs; (2) facilitating the formulation of working hypotheses with regard to major factors affecting the size of TFP and its growth pattern, thereby promoting a better understanding of the production process; (3) assessing the welfare implications of variations of TFP in terms of changes in the total pie available for distribution at the economy, industry, and company levels; (4) monitoring potential for changes in relative performance levels of companies and industries (e.g., profitability, growth, competitiveness) and the economy (e.g., inflation, employment, living standards, international trade); and (5) managing government enterprises and regulated industries on the basis of production efficiencies. At the same time, the study of the TFP residual is likely to advance our knowledge of the production systems of our business.

2 PRODUCTIVITY INDEXES, PRODUCTION FUNCTIONS, COST FUNCTIONS AND TECHNICAL CHANGE

TFP Indexes Production Functions and Technical Change

Conceptually, there is little difference between production function studies and productivity studies. Both specify implicitly or explicitly the structure of the production system to be studied. Solow (1957) has shown that productivity analysis, in a production theory context, could be viewed as a decomposition of the production process to movements along the production function (expansion of output due to input augmentation) and shifts of the production function (technical change). Viewed from this angle, and assuming a single-output production system, the production function can be written as:

$$Y = f(X_1, X_2, \ldots, X_i, \ldots, X_n, t) \tag{2.1}$$

where Y is output, X_i is the i-th input and t is a technology variable that represents the shift in the production function over time or technical change. Assuming that technical change is Hicks-neutral (i.e., technological innovations do not affect the technically optimal ratio among the inputs), differentiating Y totally with respect to time, we obtain:

$$\frac{dY}{dt} = \sum_{i=1}^{n} \frac{\partial Y}{\partial X_i}\frac{\partial X_i}{\partial t} + \frac{\partial Y}{\partial t} \tag{2.2}$$

denoting $\dot{Y} = (dY/dt)$, $\dot{X}_i = (\partial X_i/\partial t)$ we get:

$$\dot{Y} = \sum_{i=1}^{n} \frac{\partial Y}{\partial X_i}\dot{X}_i + \frac{\partial Y}{\partial t} \tag{2.3}$$

Rearranging (2.3) to solve for the elasticity of technical change with respect to output, $\dot{A}$, and multiplying and dividing the first term on the left hand expression in (2.3) by X_i we get:

$$\dot{A} = \frac{\partial \dot{Y}}{\partial t}\frac{1}{Y} = \frac{\dot{Y}}{Y} - \sum_{i=1}^{n} \frac{\partial Y}{\partial X_i}\frac{X_i}{Y}\frac{\dot{X}_i}{X_i} \tag{2.4}$$

where $\dot{A}$ can be interpreted as the percentage change in output induced by a small percentage change in technology.

Assuming that the firm is pursuing profit maximization by equating the value of the marginal product of each input to its price, we substitute $(\partial Y)/(\partial X_i) = W_i/P$, for all i into (2.4) to obtain:

$$\dot{A} = \frac{\dot{Y}}{Y} - \sum_{i=1}^{n} \frac{W_i X_i \dot{X}_i}{PYX_i} = \frac{\dot{Y}}{Y} - \sum_{i=1}^{n} \alpha_i \frac{\dot{X}_i}{X_i}\,. \tag{2.5}$$

where $\alpha_i = \Sigma_{i=1}^{n}(W_i X_i/PY)$ is the share of the total costs of the i-th input in total revenues, or total costs, given that $PY = \Sigma_{i=1}^{n} W_i X_i$.

The technical change continuous expression for $\dot{A}$ in (2.5) is analogous to the Divisia continuous expression for TFP change (see equation 1.5). The sum of the cost shares is unity ($\Sigma_{i=1}^{n}\ \alpha_i = 1$), and the underlying production function for (2.5) exhibits constant returns to scale, i.e., an equi-proportional change in all inputs induces the same proportional change in output.

The production function in (2.5) can be estimated either econometrically or through computation of TFP indexes. One important empirical advantage of TFP indexes is that they do not require resort to statistical estimation techniques mandated by econometric approaches. The latter commonly involve the use of a variety of least-square methods whose proper specification makes it necessary to assume that all systematic explanatory factors have been properly accounted for. This defies the rationale behind the concept of TFP as a residual measure of our ignorance. In view of our generally limited knowledge of complex production processes such complete and accurate specification of all systematic explanatory variables and full-characterization of the nature of technical change are often unattainable. As a result, econometric analyses of production functions may produce estimates of production parameters of questionable statistical quality and economic meaning.

Econometric specifications of production models require direct measurements of technical change which in the construction of productivity indexes is treated as part of the unexplained residual. Time is very often used as a crude proxy for technical change in econometric production models. However, the conceptualization of technical change as a shift in the production function over time regardless of its inherent limitations does not imply that the use of a time index as a proxy for the specification of technical change is necessarily valid. Time as a technical change variable portrays very smooth and monotonous rates of change in the impact of technical change on output and invariably excludes cycles and reinforcing chain effects in the diffusion of innovations.

On a micro level, adequate specification of technical change inputs in production function research requires detailed engineering knowledge of the technical innovation process. Such knowledge is rarely available at the production center level, let alone at a corporate or industry level basis. At best, complete engineering characterization of technology inputs may be possible for very specific disaggregate production processes. It is for these micro quasi-engineering production systems that the econometric production function may be a most helpful auxiliary tool.

Apart from the problem of the appropriate proxy for technology, correct econometric specification of the technological structure requires precise distinction between embodied and disembodied technical change, as well as between scale-related and scale-independent technical change. Anything short of relatively precise characterization of technology may impair the economic and statistical validity and reliability of empirical findings.

Numerous attempts have been made at specifications of embodied technology, mainly through input augmentation (see Nerlove, 1963; Beckman and Sato, 1969; Fishelson, 1977). Most of these specifications use relatively crude proxies for augmentation, with potentially adverse effects on the quality of the findings. TFP index measurements allow for embodied effects only through changes in input prices that in turn change the weights assigned for aggregation. Increase in input quality would presumably increase its price by increasing the average and marginal product associated with its use. This does not in general adequately account for the effects of embodied technical change.

Yet errors resulting from imperfect specifications may be easier to identify in TFP index measurements than in econometric production function estimation, since the former do not contain errors due to weaknesses inherent in the application of statistical methods.

In principle, econometric estimation of production functions can accommodate multi-output multi-input structures by resorting to the use of multivariate statistical estimation techniques, such as factor analysis, principle component analysis, and canonical correlation (see Vinod, 1968, 1976). In practice, the resulting multivariate estimates are often unstable because of the prevalence of strong multicollinearity among the input and output series. This problem can be alleviated to some extent by Vinod's (1976) proposal to use canonical ridge (joint application of ridge regression and canonical correlation). For TFP indexes, a multi-output specification poses no problem. In fact, proper disaggregation of outputs increases the reliability of TFP measurements.

TFP Indexes, Cost Functions and Technical Change

Productivity changes can be interpreted as shifts in the production function. By the same logic, productivity changes could be viewed as shifts in the cost function. This follows directly from the fundamental duality relationships between cost and production structures.

Consider a cost function specification of the following type:

$$C = g(\bar{Y}, \bar{W}, t) \tag{2.6}$$

where C denotes total costs, and $\bar{Y}$ and $\bar{W}$ are outputs and input price vectors respectively. Note that the cost function formulation (2.6) affords estimation of the multi-output without resorting to multivariate statistical methods.

On theoretical grounds, a direct cost function estimation of productivity changes is somewhat preferable to a direct production function estimation. The former allows for an endogenous treatment of input prices in the production decision, while the latter method does not, Nonetheless, direct cost function estimations pose additional statistical problems because a subset of the explanatory variables (the outputs) is stochastic, and because of the large number of independent variables (outputs and input prices). Both production and cost function estimation can accommodate multi-output specifications, but direct cost estimation in a multi-output case is advantageous in the sense that, unlike production estimation, it can be achieved by the specification of a single dependent variable.

Using the cost function approach, we can, following Denny et al. (1981), be more specific about the relationship between total factor productivity, technical change and pricing procedures. Defining $(1/C)\cdot(\partial g/\partial t)$, as a factor shift in the cost function, differentiating (2.6) totally with respect to time and rearranging Denny et al., obtain:

$$\dot{\text{TFP}} = -\frac{1}{C}\frac{\partial g}{\partial t} + (1 - \sum_j \varepsilon_{cy_j})\dot{Y}^C + (\dot{Y}^P - \dot{Y}^C) \qquad (2.7)$$

where $\varepsilon_{cy_j} = (Y_j/C)\cdot(\partial C/\partial Y_j)$ is the total cost elasticity with respect to the j-th output, $\dot{Y}_j = (1/Y)\cdot(\partial Y_j/\partial t)$, $\dot{Y}^P = \Sigma_j[\{(P_j Y_j)/(\Sigma_j P_j Y_j)\cdot(\dot{Y}_j)]$ is the growth of total output over time with each individual output Y_j weighted by the share of revenues $P_j Y_j$ it generates out of total revenues $\Sigma_j P_j Y_j$. $\dot{Y}^c = \Sigma_j[\{(\varepsilon_{cy_i})/(\Sigma_j \varepsilon_{cy_j})\}\cdot(\dot{Y}_j)]$ is the growth in total output obtained by using cost elasticities shares in aggregating growths of individual outputs.

The expression in (2.7) partitions total factor productivity growth to three components: (a) Hick neutral technical change, represented by the downward shift in the cost function $(1/C)\cdot(\partial g/\partial t)$; (b) the effects of economies of scale $(1 - \Sigma_j \varepsilon_{cy_j})$; and (c) the effects of departure from marginal cost pricing $(\dot{Y}^P - \dot{Y}^C)$. If the firm follows marginal cost pricing (i.e., $P_j = \partial C/\partial Y_j$ for all j), then it can be shown that $\dot{Y}^P = \dot{Y}^C$. The third term in (2.7) disappears and TFP growth is equal to the combined effects of technical change and scale. Furthermore, under constant returns to scale $\Sigma_j \varepsilon_{cy_j} = 1$ and the second term in (2.7) disappears. It follows that only if a firm minimizes costs, exhibits constant returns to scale in production and engages in marginal cost pricing, will the growth in total factor productivity equal its Hick's neutral technical change. In the case of nonconstant returns to scale productivity growth captures both technical and scale effects.

In the nonregulated sectors only firms operating in perfectly competitive markets maximize profits via marginal cost pricing. Consequently, conventional TFP Divisia indexes are likely to be biased for monopolies and oligopolies. This ties in with our discussion of productivity indexes in chapter 1. The direct derivation of TFP Divisia indexes is predicated on the assumption that changes in the quantities of inputs and outputs are independent of the respective prices (i.e., competitive output and input markets) and the uniqueness of discrete measures of TFP change is guaranteed by the prevalence of profit maximizing behavior in competitive markets. Regulated firms may deviate from marginal cost pricing either because of regulatory policy or through regulatory default. Thus, the TFP measure for regulated monopolies and oligopolies may show a bias whenever it captures effects of deviations from marginal cost pricing in addition to scale and technical effects. The magnitude of this bias is given by the $\dot{Y}^P - \dot{Y}^C$ term in (2.7). The direction of the bias is generally unknown a priori, but can be computed once marginal costs are estimated.

Specific Functional Forms and TFP Indexes

Econometric analysis of production and cost functions require specifications of explicit functional forms so that their parameters can be statistically estimated. To this end, it is useful to choose a flexible functional form; i.e., a function that is general enough to provide a reasonable approximation for many specific functions. One such widely used form is the transcendental logarithmic (translog function) proposed by Christensen et al. (1971, 1973). Within the general single-output production function framework in (2.1) the translog production function can be written as follows:

$$\ln Y = \ln a_0 + \sum_{i=1}^{n} a_i \ln X_i + 1/2 \sum_{i=1}^{n} \sum_{j=1}^{m} a_{ij} \ln X_i \ln X_j \qquad (2.8)$$

where $a_{ij} = a_{ji}$.

The translog form in (2.8) is fairly generally in the sense that it can be shown, via Taylor series expansion, to be a second-order local approximation to any arbitrary twice differentiable logarithmic function. This property of the translog obviously reduces the likelihood of the quality of the estimates of the production parameters being adversely affected by the restrictiveness of more conventional functional forms.

Note that a direct estimation of the translog production function in (2.8) does not require any restrictive assumptions about competitive markets, profit maximizing behavior, constant returns to scale or the neutrality of technical change. The inputs in (2.8) include technology variables as a subset of the input set $\{X_1, \ldots, X_i, \ldots, X_n\}$. The parameters of cross products of technology inputs and ordinary inputs in translog functions reflect patterns of embodied technical change by capturing the effects on output of the interactions between levels of inputs and technology.

Direct estimation of (2.8) however may be spurious at times because it implicitly assumes that production decisions are made on technical grounds only, without being affected by levels and changes in input prices. This assumption may not always accurately portray the behavior of profit oriented firms in a dynamic world characterized by frequent changes in relative input prices. One way to remedy the problem is to construct a simultaneous model consisting of production function and factor demand equations (see for example Eldor et al., (1979)). However, this simultaneous equation procedure calls for specification of explicit input demand function and thus requires some prior knowledge of the effects of embodied technical change, as well as input prices on the demanded quantities of inputs.

Statistical estimation of the translog form in (2.8) may prove a difficult task. Even if only a small number of inputs is specified, the number of independent variables becomes fairly large which, in turn, necessitates a large number of data observations. Furthermore, the likelihood for high degrees of systematic interdependence among the independent variables (multicollinearity) increases with the number of those explanatory variables. To overcome the fuzziness that multi-collinearity introduces into the statistical and economic interpretation of the results, more elaborate statistical estimation techniques (e.g., ridge regression) may have to be used. Regardless of the sophistication and complexity of the estimation techniques used, a completely satisfactory treatment of multicollinearity problems is yet to be found.

For manageable estimation simplification of the production function in (2.8) often requires additional restrictive assumptions. For example, if it is reasonable to assume that technical change is Hick neutral and the underlying production function exhibits constant returns to scale then the translog expression in (2.8) can be reduced to:

$$\ln Y = \ln a_0 + \sum_{i=1}^{n} a_i \ln X_i + 1/2 \sum_{i=1}^{n} \sum_{j=1}^{n} a_{ij} \ln X_i \ln X_j + a_t \ln t \qquad (2.9)$$

where the inputs $\{X_1, \ldots, X_i, \ldots, X_n\}$ do *not* include technology inputs. t is the technology index, and a_t is the elasticity of output with respect to technology. Thus, the two ordinary input terms in (2.9) could be viewed as the underlying aggregator function for the inputs (i.e., the functional rule that transforms the individual inputs into an aggregate (total) input expression). The total input is then transformed into output by the scalar technology index t.

Diewert (1976) has shown that a constant returns to scale translog total input aggregator function is the only differentiable linear homogeneous function which is exact for the Törnqvist discrete form of quantity Divisia index. This means that there is a unique correspondence between linearly homogeneous translog input and output aggregator functions and the expressions for total inputs and output is the Tornquist discrete approximation to a TFP Divisia index, as expressed in equation (1.7). Thus, it can be argued that within the confines of constant returns to scale and neutral technical change the underlying aggregator functions for the total input and total output aggregates of a Divisia TFP index are fairly general.

The basic importance of these results lies in the linkage established between the TFP index approach and the econometric approach to productivity measurement. The selection of an appropriate production function and a suitable index number for measuring technical change were found to be related in the sense that the use of a certain TFP index implies certain implicit underlying production functions and output aggregator functions. For example, a choice of a Laspeyres TFP index has been shown to imply an underlying linear production function in which all inputs are perfect substitutes in the production process.

A translog cost function is also widely used in the estimation of technical change. Based on the general cost function specification in (2.6) the explicit translog functional formulation can provide a second-order approximation for any arbitrary variable cost function. If we are willing to assume that the firm minimizes costs we can invoke Shephard's lemma and derive (by differentiating the cost function with respect to input prices) a system of input demand equations. Such input demand equations, if derived from a translog cost function, greatly facilitate statistical estimation by reducing the complexity of the functional forms and the number of independent variables.

Translog production and cost functions, although widely used, are by no means the only generalized functional forms suitable for productivity analysis. A number of other general functional forms have been proposed recently. Prominent among them are the generalized Leontief function, the generalized Cobb-Douglas function and the generalized square-root quadratic. Khaled (1978) proposed the generalized Box-Cox functional form which takes on all the other forms including the translog as special or limit cases. All these functional forms are general in the sense that they place few a priori restrictions on patterns of relationships among inputs or between inputs and outputs. They are also flexible in the sense that they can be interpreted as second order approximations to arbitrary production or cost functions. Nonetheless, a choice among these general functions is not easy since empirical results can vary substantially depending on the particular functional form chosen, in spite of its generality. Consequently, in selecting explicit functions, analysts may have to resort to some prior knowledge of production and cost relationships. In the absence of reliable prior information it may be prudent to estimate several generalized functional forms and select the specifications that generates either the most sensible economic results and/or the best statistical estimates. Nonetheless, parametric productivity estimates which are very sensitive to alternative specifications of underlying functional forms ought to be treated with caution.

Some Empirical Macro–Economic Observations

Numerous macro-economic productivity studies have been conducted during the postwar period. Estimates of productivity performance of major sectors of national economies and key industries are publicly available. Published productivity studies of individual companies are relatively rare. Corporate productivity data is generally viewed as strategically sensitive and therefore usually classified as confidential. In this section we provide a very brief and very partial survey of empirical productivity studies on the macro-economic level. One of the objectives is to highlight the degree of sensitivity of productivity results to alternative measures and estimation methods.

Table 2-1 summarizes TFP growth results of selected productivity studies of the U.S. economy. Caution should be exercised in comparing these results because of the different periods covered. Also, the sectors of the economy for which TFP is measured are not always strictly comparable. For example, the Brendt and Khaled (1979) findings pertain to the U.S. manufacturing sector, while the Bureau of Labor Statistics (1983) figures are for the U.S. private domestic economy. The BLS annual TFP growth rate computed for manufacturing during 1948–1981 is 1.81%. However, most significant differences in TFP estimates for comparable periods seem to be largely attributable to the sensitivity of the findings to measurement techniques and estimation methods.

Solow (1957), Christensen and Jorgenson (1970), Star (1974), Hulten (1979), and the Bureau of Labor Statistics (1983) used TFP Divisia indexes for which the implicit underlying production function is a constant returns to

Table 2-1. Total Factor Productivity Growth in the U.S. Economy (Selected Studies)

Study	*Period*	*% Annual Growth in TFP*
Abramovitz (1956)	1869–1953	1.0%
Solow (1957)	1909–1949	1.5%
Christensen and Jorgenson (1970)	1929–1967	1.13%
Denison (1974)	1929–1969	1.5%
Star (1974)	1950–1960	1.5%
Hulten (1979)	1948–1966	1.5%*
	1948–1966	2.8%**
Brendt and Khaled (1979)	1947–1971	0.7%
Kendrick (1980)	1889–1919	1.7%
	1919–1948	2.2%
	1948–1978	2.3%
Bureau of Labor Statistics (1983)	1948–1981	1.5%

*Conventional TFP residual.
**Dynamic TFP residual.

scale translog function. By contrast, Abramovitz (1956), Denison (1974) and Kendrick (1980) used Laspeyres TFP indexes which are consistent with a constant return to scale, constant elasticity of substitution production function. Denison employed a growth accounting approach with an underlying additive production function. Brendt and Khaled (1979) used a parametric approach based on a generalized Box-Cox production function.

Jorgenson and Griliches (1967) and Christensen and Jorgenson (1969) introduced significant changes in input and output measurements relative to the techniques used by Abramovitz, Denison and Kendrick. Among the major changes in input and output measurements were (a) disaggregation of capital stock measurements; (b) imputation of capital users' cost weights; (c) adjustments for utilization of capital, and (d) inclusion of purchases of consumer durables in the investment component of output and the imputed value of these services in consumption.

Generally speaking, it may be argued that given the differences in the structures of the underlying models, as well as in the methods of measuring outputs and inputs, the relative closeness of the TFP results is surprising. All researchers found significant productivity growth in the U.S. throughout the first part of the twentieth century and the postwar period. There are however significant differences of opinion as to how much of this growth is attributable to economies of scale vs. technical change. Findings by Jorgenson and Griliches (1967) and Brendt and Khaled (1979) suggest that a relatively small portion of the TFP residual is attributable to neutral technical change, and most of the advances in productivity are attributable to economies of scale. Denison's results on the other hand assign a much larger role to neutral technical change. These differences have important policy and managerial implications. If productivity improvements are largely dependent on the scale of operations than slower real growth of industrial enterprises and the economy at large is likely to impede productivity growth. From this viewpoint, it may not be surprising that all macro-economic productivity studies show a pronounced deceleration in U.S. productivity growth in the seventies, coinciding with lower rates of growth in real output during the same decade. Yet, the general debate over the cause and effect of such relationships is far from being settled. For example, it is unclear whether decline in the rate of growth in productivity attributable to lower real economic growth, or whether both can be traced to fewer innovations and slower progress in research and development. The TFP residual remains a measure of our ignorance. Attempts to explain this residual away by vigorous identification of the major factors behind TFP growth and their relative impact met so far with little scientific success.

Hulten (1979) developed an effective measure of TFP change inclusive of the productivity-induced accumulation of capital which he terms dynamic residual. This dynamic residual, in contrast to the conventional residual, allows for the effects of capital accumulation by treating investment as an intermediate good and consumption as the only direct delivery of final demand. Applying this model to Christensen's and Jorgenson's data, Hulten found that the dynamic TFP grew at almost double the rate of the conventional TFP (see table 2-1), and that the dynamic residual accounted for 66% of the rate of growth in real additions to wealth (income used for consumption) compared with 38% for the conventional residual. Thus, Hulten, following Hicks and Rymes, makes a strong argument for the need to measure technical change in a dynamic (capital endogenous) framework. Certainly this could be regarded as a more appropriate approach to measure TFP's contributions to long term growth in wealth and economic well-being. The conventional residual may significantly understate the portion of growth attributable to technical change by failing to account for the reproducibility of capital and its productivity inducing effects. By the same logic, the dynamic residual may be also a more appropriate measure of the contributions of productivity gains to the wealth of the firm. So far, we know of no attempt to apply this methodology to the measurement of company productivity.

The sensitivity of TFP measures to levels of input aggregation is demonstrated by Star (1974). Disaggregation of the capital stock into structures and equipment and the labor force by sex, occupation, age, education and race reduces the role of the conventional TFP residual in real value-added output growth from 47% to 27% and TFP's annual rate of growth from 1.51% to 0.87%. However, as noted by Star, these results should not necessarily be interpreted as suggestive of a radically diminished role of technical change as an explanatory factor behind growth: "The reduction of residual growth does not eliminate technological progress as an important causal factor in growth. The changing structure of the labor force, a factor emphasized in this paper, is a result in large part, of the forces of technological progress. The residual is a measure of our ignorance about only one aspect of growth." (Star (1974) p. 134)

One of the theoretically most attractive TFP estimation methods is the parametric approach used by Brendt and Khaled (1979). They estimated TFP growth directly from parameters of the generalized Box-Cox cost function rather than from a simple residual of growth in outputs minus growth in inputs. Testing for the validity of less general functional forms, Brendt and Khaled found for annual U.S. manufacturing data 1947–71 that the generalized square root quadratic function must be rejected, but that the generalized Leontief function cannot be rejected as a special case of the Box-Cox model. Their results also suggest rejection of models reasonably close to the translog limiting case. Further empirical tests reject the constant returns to scale hypothesis. Technical change has been found by Brendt and Khaled to be significantly capital and energy using. Thus the neutral technical change hypothesis is also rejected, although not as decisively as the constant returns to scale hypothesis. In this context, it is noteworthy that the TFP annual growth estimate of 0.7% attributed to Brendt and Khaled in table 2-1 was obtained by imposing the (rejected) constant returns to scale and neutrality of technical change assumptions. If those assumptions are relaxed, then significant economies of scale are discerned and the annual rate of TFP growth falls significantly.

Empirical Study of Major U.S. Industrial Groups

Kendrick and Grossman (1980) estimated TFP growth in the U.S. by major industry groups throughout the postwar period. Their results are summarized in table 2-2. These findings represent updating of earlier industry studies by Kendrick and are based on Laspeyres TFP residual measurements. The TFP growth estimates in table 2-2 highlight pronounced differences in productivity performances among industry. For the 1948–1976 period TFP growth for industries ranged from annual rates close to 4% to close to zero. The impact of productivity gains on prices of products and services is obvious. The rate of growth in the implicit price deflator for each industry in table 2-2 is approximately equal to the difference between the rates of growth in average factor prices and total factor productivity for the same industry. This underscores the role of productivity growth in attenuating cost increases and maintaining the competitiveness of industries and firms.

The sensitivity of TFP growth rates to changes in business conditions and business cycles is illustrated in table 2-3. Note for example, that the productivity performance of the primary metals industry groups has been much more sensitive to business cycles than productivity performance in communications.

In general, it is hardly surprising that the more cyclical industries show the greatest variability in TFP growth. Since input adjustments and capacity adjustments lag behind abrupt and unforeseen changes in demand, it is understandable that mining, railroads, lumber, paper and public utilities suffered the sharpest productivity setbacks during the 1973–1976 period of strong stagflation. The results in table 2-3 also underscore the importance of

Table 2-2. Changes in Unit Factor Costs, and Product Prices by Major Industry Group (Average Annual Percentage Rates of Change: 1948-76)

	Implicit Product Price Deflator	*Unit Factor Cost*	*Average Factor Price*	*Total Factor Productivity*
Farming	1.7	1.6	4.7	3.0
Manufacturing	2.8	2.9	5.0	2.1
Food	2.2	2.6	5.5	2.9
Tobacco	1.8	4.7	7.3	2.6
Textile	0.1	0.1	3.1	3.1
Apparel	1.5	1.5	4.0	2.5
Lumber	2.9	3.0	6.0	2.9
Furniture	2.9	2.8	4.7	1.8
Paper	2.9	2.8	4.9	2.0
Printing and publishing	3.5	3.5	5.1	1.5
Chemical	1.5	1.4	4.6	3.2
Petroleum	1.6	0.5	2.5	2.1
Rubber	2.9	3.2	5.0	1.8
Leather	2.9	2.8	4.0	1.1
Stone, clay, and glass	3.7	3.7	5.0	1.3
Primary metals	5.2	5.1	5.2	0.1
Fabricated Metals	3.6	3.8	5.3	1.3
Nonelectrical machinery	3.8	3.8	4.9	1.7
Electrical machinery	1.2	1.3	5.1	3.7
Transportation equipment	2.5	2.7	5.5	2.7
Instruments	2.8	3.3	6.7	2.2
Miscellaneous	2.0	2.0	4.7	2.7
Nonfarm and Nonmanufacturing	3.3	3.2	5.2	2.0
Mining	3.7	3.5	5.2	1.7
Construction	4.2	4.2	5.3	1.0
Transportation, total	3.0	3.0	5.5	2.4
Railroads	2.2	2.4	4.9	2.5
Nonrail	3.9	3.8	5.4	1.6
Communications	2.0	2.3	6.7	4.2
Public utilities	2.5	2.5	5.6	3.0
Trade	2.9	2.6	4.7	2.1
Finance and insurance	4.7	4.5	4.7	0.1
Real estate	3.2	3.0	5.9	2.8
Services	4.4	4.4	6.1	1.6
Total	3.0	2.9	5.3	2.3

Source: Kendrick (1980).

Table 2-3. Average Annual Percentage Rates of Change of Total Tangible Factor Productivity by Industry Group

	1948–73	*1948–53*	*1953–57*	*1957–60*	*1960–66*	*1966–69*	*1969–73*	*1973–76*
Business economy	2.5	3.4	2.0	2.1	3.4	1.5	1.8	0.7
Farm	3.3	5.4	2.7	3.8	2.3	3.2	3.3	1.1
Manufacturing	2.3	2.9	1.0	1.1	3.9	0.9	2.7	0.1
Food	2.8	3.3	2.5	1.1	4.0	1.1	2.8	3.8
Tobacco	2.7	1.1	3.5	4.8	2.0	3.6	3.0	1.1
Textiles	3.3	0.8	3.6	1.9	8.2	0.1	2.7	0.7
Apparel	2.5	2.8	1.4	1.2	2.0	0.8	5.5	2.5
Lumber	3.8	0.4	5.7	1.5	7.2	1.6	4.9	−4.7
Furniture	1.9	2.2	2.7	0.1	2.7	2.0	1.0	0.8
Paper	2.7	3.7	−0.4	1.7	2.8	2.7	5.3	−3.5
Printing and publishing	1.9	2.2	2.8	0.6	3.1	0.2	0.7	−1.0
Chemical	3.6	1.8	0.6	5.4	4.1	0.8	2.3	−1.7
Petroleum	2.5	1.8	0.6	5.4	4.1	0.8	2.3	−1.7
Rubber	2.1	2.1	−2.3	5.7	3.6	3.2	1.4	−1.5
Leather	1.1	−2.0	0.7	3.0	3.1	−0.3	2.1	1.2

Stone, clay, and glass	1.6	2.4	0.1	1.1	2.4	0.8	1.7	−0.9
Primary metals	0.6	3.2	−1.5	−4.1	3.3	−3.1	1.8	−3.9
Fabricated metals	1.5	1.4	0.3	2.0	2.6	1.5	0.9	−0.9
Nonelectrical machinery	1.3	2.5	−1.1	1.1	2.6	−0.2	2.3	−0.5
Electrical machinery	3.9	4.4	2.0	2.6	1.2	2.9	3.7	1.6
Transportation equipment	2.6	3.2	1.5	3.3	4.2	−0.5	2.7	3.0
Instruments	2.5	4.6	0.6	3.0	3.5	3.1	−0.4	0.1
Miscellaneous	2.8	4.0	3.3	2.6	1.6	3.1	2.8	1.6
Mining	2.4	4.1	2.2	0.6	4.6	1.7	0.7	−4.6
Contract construction	0.9	2.6	1.8	4.2	2.0	−0.3	−5.0	1.8
Railroads	3.2	2.5	2.6	4.2	7.0	1.3	0.2	−3.6
Nonrail transportation	1.8	0.4	2.1	1.2	2.6	1.9	2.8	1.2
Communications	4.2	5.7	4.5	5.9	3.5	3.4	2.5	4.3
Public utilities	3.9	6.8	4.7	4.6	3.7	2.7	0.2	−3.8
Trade	2.4	2.1	1.6	1.8	3.6	1.0	2.9	—
Real estate	2.8	4.4	2.9	3.8	2.6	1.3	1.3	3.1

Source: Kendrick (1980).

distinguishing between long-term and short-term productivity performance for planning and decision making purposes.

Selected Empirical Observations on the Company Level

Denny's et al. (1981) study of the productivity of Bell Canada provides a very interesting example of a productivity analysis of an individual company using the TFP index (residual) approach, combined with a cost function (parametric) methodology. Their results with regard to the sources of TFP growth in Canadian telecommunications according to the decomposition formula outlined in equation (2.7) are presented in table 2-4. The shift in the translog cost function associated with technical change, $(1/C)(\partial g/\partial t)$, was traced to (a) the introduction and diffusion of direct dialing, and to (b) modern switching facilities. According to Denny et al., nonmarginal cost pricing and technical change each account for approximately 20% of conventionally measured TFP during the 1952–76 period, while increasing returns to scale account for about 60% for the same period. The two major technological innovations, which represent technical change in this study, contributed approximately equally to TFP growth over the entire period. Direct distance dialing however was more important in the earlier period, and modern switching more important in the latter period. The source of the residual is regression error resulting from the need to estimate cost elasticities and technical change effects via a cost function approach in accordance with equation (2.7). The residual from estimation is relatively large in individual subperiods but averages out over the whole period.

In the same study, Denny et al. also compute parametric total factor productivity growth estimates directly from the estimated cost function. This methodology is similar in principle to the Brendt and Khaled (1979) approach, except that the cost function used for Bell Canada data is the translog instead of the generalized Box-Cox form. In computing the parametric TFP growth, the effects of departure from marginal cost pricing and the unexplained estimation residual on total factor productivity growth were excluded. A comparison between the conventional (residually) measured TFP growth results and the parametric TFP growth estimates are presented in table 2-5.

Friedlaender et al. (1983) analyzed the productivity performance of the big three U.S. automobile manufacturers. They obtain parametric measures of productivity by specifying a general hedonic joint cost function representing a second order Taylor nonlogarithmic approximation around the mean. A large number of zero outputs for small cars in the earlier period

Table 2-4. Sources of Conventionally Measured Total Factor Productivity Growth for Bell Canada Parametric Technical Changes

		Percentage contributions to TFP growth of				
			Efficiency gains due to			
				Shift of the cost function associated with		
Time Period	*Residually determined total factor productivity growth (%)*	*Nonmarginal Cost Pricing*	*Nonconstant returns to scale*	*Access to direct-distance dialing*	*Connection to modern switching facilities*	*Residual from estimation*
1952–1957	1.25	29.9	28.4	14.0	14.1	13.5
1958–1962	3.01	6.7	42.8	35.4	12.2	3.0
1963–1966	3.09	24.7	64.2	10.2	17.6	−16.7
1967–1970	4.66	13.6	62.9	2.5	10.0	11.0
1971–1976	4.46	15.7	83.9	0.5	8.4	−8.6
1952–1976	3.35	16.0	63.7	10.2	11.4	−1.3

Source: Denny et al. (1981).

Table 2-5. A Comparison of Two Measures of Total Factor Productivity Growth for Bell Canada

Time Period	*Residually determined total factor productivity growth TFP (%)*	*Parametric total factor productivity growth TFP* (%)*
1952–1957	1.25	0.71
1958–1962	3.01	2.72
1963–1966	3.09	2.85
1967–1970	4.66	3.51
1971–1976	4.46	4.14
1952–1976	3.35	2.81

Source: Denny et al. (1981).

Table 2-6. Notation of Variables Used in Estimation of Cost Functions of U.S. Automobile Manufacturers

Notation	*Variable*
C	total cost of domestic production per year (in million dollars)
y_1	small car production per year (subcompact and compact)
y_2	large car production per year (full-size and luxury)
y_3	truck production per year
q_{11}	wheel base of small car (in inches)
q_{12}	weight of small car (in pounds)
q_{13}	cylinder capacity of small car (in cubic inches)
q_{21}	wheelbase of large car (in inches)
q_{22}	weight of large car (in pounds)
q_{23}	cylinder capacity of large car (in cubic inches)
q_{31}	weight of truck (in pounds)
w_1	labor price (in dollars per hour)
w_2	capital price (in percent per dollar per year)
w_3	materials price (in dollars per ton)
T	dummy variable for time

Source: Friedlaender et al. (1983).

Table 2-7. Productivity Change for General Motors, Ford, and Chrysler, 1969-1979

	General Motors		*Ford*		*Chrysler*	
Year	$\frac{\partial C}{\partial T}$ *(mil.)*	$\frac{\partial C}{\partial T}$ *(%)*	$\frac{\partial C}{\partial T}$ *(mil.)*	$\frac{\partial C}{\partial T}$ *(%)*	$\frac{\partial C}{\partial T}$ *(mil.)*	$\frac{\partial C}{\partial T}$ *(%)*
1979	−272.771	−.53	−433.09	−1.54	904.22	7.81
1978	−690.627	−1.40	−643.88	−2.35	579.41	4.69
1977	−447.011	−1.03	308.15	−1.27	595.34	4.05
1976	2.6373	.007	−38.78	−.21	430.97	3.21
1975	−241.303	−.84	−6.78	−.04	611.43	5.88
1974	814.777	3.14	−149.53	−.93	268.72	2.76
1973	13.4968	.05	−214.75	−1.40	245.10	2.41
1972	−239.038	−.97	−140.50	−1.03	226.93	2.68
1971	−137.479	−.60	−101.18	−.90	350.89	4.90
1970	202.399	1.26	−363.12	−3.54	366.32	5.70
1969	147.01	.73	−487.59	−4.82	459.46	7.12

Source: Friedlaender et al. (1983).

observations of the data sample precluded the use of the translog cost function, and a relatively small number of observations in general precluded the use of a Box-Cox transformation in a translog specification which is usually designed to circumvent the problem of zero values. The variables used in the estimation of the cost function are given in table 2-6 where the y variables are the outputs, the q variables are the qualities associated with the relevant outputs, and the w variables are the input prices. Shephard's lemma was used to derive the factor demand equation for each input.

By differentiating the estimated cost-function with respect to time, Friedlaender et al. estimated productivity growth patterns for General Motors, Ford, and Chrysler which are presented in table 2-7. Productivity changes are represented by shifts in the cost function, with productivity gains evident only if $\partial C/\partial T$ is negative. Their results indicate that Ford, and to some extent General Motors, have enjoyed productivity growth for the majority of the past decade. Chrysler on the other hand has experienced substantial cost increases and productivity decreases during this same period. Friedlaender et al. also found in separate tests that General Motors' and Chrysler's production structures were subject to significant economies of scale, while Ford's operations exhibited significant diseconomies of scale.

The authors point out that "these results are important since they suggest that even if Chrysler did not suffer a competitive disadvantage with respect to its recent scale of production, it would still be at a competitive disadvantage vis-à-vis Ford and General Motors because of its recent poor productivity." (Friedlaender et al. (1983) p. 18) It is interesting to speculate whether Chrysler's executives could have averted financial crisis by initiating preemptive corrective actions based on information from similar comparative productivity studies had they been able to conduct such studies in the early seventies.

3 EFFICIENCY AND EFFECTIVENESS

The Relationships Between Technical Efficiency and Effectiveness

Understanding of the relationship between technical efficiency and effectiveness is crucial for sound managerial planning and decision making. In a world of incomplete information, an operation can be highly efficient in terms of very impressive physical input-output (productivity) ratios, but ineffective in terms of delivering higher-level objectives. For example, a profit making firm can, due to intra-organizational conflicts, produce very efficiently an undesired product or service which will result in poor profitability. Failure to attain minimum profit goals will result in this case in low effectiveness in spite of relatively high productivity. At times, there may even be a trade off between technical efficiency and effectiveness. For example, it may be occasionally easier for the production department to improve productivity by standardizing products at the expense of neglecting customized demands, thereby adversely affecting marketability and profitability. Generally speaking, we can cite numerous examples where efficiency and effectiveness are not necessarily positively correlated. This simply illustrates that both efficiency and effectiveness have to be measured and monitored to improve goal congruency and overall organizational performance.

Technical efficiency relates to the manner in which physical resources are used to produce quantities of outputs. In this sense efficiency and productivity can be used interchangeably. Efficient production however is a means to an end, not an end in itself. Purposeful organizations strive to operate efficiently in their pursuit of higher level objectives. The concept of effectiveness relates to the manner in which these higher level objectives (e.g., survival, profitability, growth, reputation, good working conditions, service to society, service to the community) are attained. Effectiveness is thus measured by the extent and degree to which those objectives are accomplished. In ideal conditions, if efficiency targets and effectiveness goals are appropriately coordinated, attainment of higher technical efficiency ought to enhance effectiveness. This relationship however is not guaranteed even under the most favorable circumstances without careful and sound planning, management and execution, which requires, among other things, good measurements of effectiveness. Accordingly, we proceed to examine more precisely sources of conflicts between productivity and effectiveness, explore ways to define and measure effectiveness and to understand how these proposed measures of effectiveness relate to underlying measures of efficiency or productivity.[1]

Conflicts Between Productivity and Effectiveness

In a simple world of goal congruency, perfect information, costless monitoring and single minded universal pursuit of wealth maximization, conflicts between productivity and effectiveness need not arise. Private firms whose overriding objective is to maximize the wealth of their shareholders by choosing strategies that maximize present values of expected future streams of net cash flows are bound to enhance their effectiveness (market value) by improving their technical efficiency. Management of large decentralized organizations however is considerably more complex. With authority over diverse functions within organizations delegated to numerous agents with different personal objectives in an environment of incomplete information and significant monitoring costs, straightforward positive correlation between productivity targets and effectiveness goals cannot be guaranteed. An ingenious management of information flows, controls and incentives may be required to prevent production managers and engineers from improving technical efficiency at the expense of effectiveness or to contain the adverse productivity effects of certain marketing or financial strategies.

The need to meet multiple objectives is another source of potential conflict between productivity and effectiveness. In the real world most firms are compelled to pursue multiple objectives and can hardly afford the luxury of exclusive preoccupation with wealth maximization. For example, most firms inevitably and unintentionally produce some negative externalities. A negative externality is a non-saleable product or service. Chemical companies that discharge hazardous wastes or electric utilities that emit smoke as byproducts of the goods and services they produce are obvious examples. But negative production externalities are not limited only to a small number of distinct manufacturing processes. In fact, they are prevalent in the provision of most products and services. Consider unsafe features that are inevitable by-products of numerous commodities, unhealthy additives in foods or unhealthy side effects in drugs, to mention a few among many examples.

The common characteristics of all these negative externalities is they are unintentional by-products which confer negative external effects on customers and non-customers. The magnitude of these externalities is dictated by the technology or method of operation at hand. A firm solely dedicated to profit maximization has no incentive to reduce those harmful external effects as long as they do not adversely affect demand for its saleable products. In fact, more often than not, reduction or elimination of negative externalities is costly, thereby creating a disincentive for any corrective action. Thus, firms either voluntarily attenuate those adverse external effects or are forced to do so by government regulations. In either case, voluntary benevolence and social consciousness or governmental constraints force the firm to pursue multiple objectives, rather than striving exclusively toward wealth maximization. It is easy to see how in an environment that calls for trade-offs among multiple objectives certain strategies can improve technical efficiency and possibly profitability while impairing the effectiveness with which certain higher goals of controlling negative external effects are met. Alternatively, the technological requirements for the reduction of certain negative externalities may dictate choices of technologies or methods of operation which are less efficient.

Consider a firm producing two saleable products and a negative externality (e.g. a chemical and a hazardous waste element or electricity and smoke). The objectives of this firm are to exceed a certain profit target π^* and to keep the negative externality below 0^*. These two profit and externality limits define an admissible set of combinations of levels of output Y_1^A and Y_2^A which represent all the combinations of outputs of product 1 and 2 respectively which do not violate the minimum profit and externality constraints. Mathematically, this admissible set A can be defined as follows:

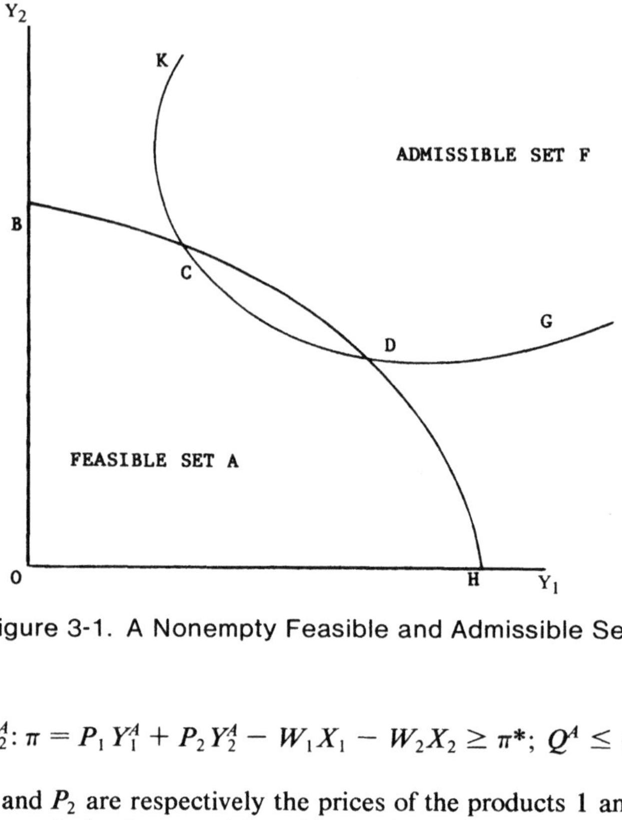

Figure 3-1. A Nonempty Feasible and Admissible Set.

$$A\{Y_1^A, Y_2^A: \pi = P_1 Y_1^A + P_2 Y_2^A - W_1 X_1 - W_2 X_2 \geq \pi^*; Q^A \leq Q^*\} \quad (3.1)$$

where P_1 and P_2 are respectively the prices of the products 1 and 2, X_1 and X_2 are respectively the quantities of input 1 and 2 and W_1 and W_2 are the respective input prices. The superscript A denotes that the $(Y_1^A; Y_2^A)$ combinations belong to the admissible objective set A. The feasibility set F is defined by the technological constraints embodied in the production function $F(Y_1^F, Y_2^F, Q^F, X_1, X_2) = 0$. Thus, the feasibility set can be mathematically defined as $F\{Y_1^F, Y_2^F: F(Y_1^F, Y_2^F, Q^F, X_1, X_2) = 0\}$. The production function F reflects a joint production of the saleable outputs Y_1 and Y_2 and the negative externality Q. The superscript F denotes that the combinations $(Y_1^F; Y_2^F)$ belong to the feasible set F. Thus, the admissible set A includes all combinations of outputs consistent with minimum acceptable levels of profits and negative external effects. The feasible set F contains all attainable combination of outputs given technology, resource limitations and budget constraints.

If the production F which represents the best available technology is known then the efficiency problem is resolved. All Y_1^F, Y_2^F combinations on the production function are by definition on the efficiency frontier and therefore represent maximum feasible productivity or efficiency, given resource constraints $X_1 \leq \bar{X}_1$, $\bar{X}_2 \leq \bar{X}_2$ or budget constraints $W_1X_1 + W_2X_2 \leq \bar{T}C$. The effectiveness problem however is resolved only if the intersection of the feasibility set F and the admissible objective set A is a non-empty set. Alternatively stated, if (Y_1, Y_2) combinations which are both feasible and admissible exist, maximum effectiveness is attained. This is illustrated in figure 3-1 where the feasible region bounded by $\overline{BCDH}$ and the admissible set by $\overline{KCDG}$. The intersection points C and D define an area contained by the CD sections of both boundaries which includes all feasible *and* admissible Y_1, Y_2 combinations. Among those, the subset of Y_1, Y_2 combination which is on the production function $F(Y_1^F, Y_2^F, Q^F, X_1, X_2) = 0$ (represented graphically by the points on the $\overline{CD}$ section of the feasibility frontier $\overline{BCDH}$) includes all admissible combinations of maximum efficiency. The actual combination to be chosen out of all points in this subset depends on the management trade-offs between Y_1 and Y_2. If for example the firms strive to maximize profits subject to a minimum acceptable externality level, it will choose of all the points on the CD section of $\overline{BCDH}$ the Y_1, Y_2 combination that maximizes π.

The Measurement of Effectiveness

If none of the admissible Y_1 Y_2 combinations are feasible the intersection between the F and A sets will be an empty set. This situation is illustrated graphically in figure 3-2. In this case, all the maximum efficiency points on the $BCDH$ feasibility boundary are ineffective in the sense that no output combinations meet minimally acceptable profit and externality control objectives. The distance between the boundaries of the feasible and admissible set represents a conceptually logical measure of effectiveness. We propose the following Euclidian distance measure of the degree of effectiveness E:[2]

$$E = 1 - \frac{\sqrt{(Y_1^A - Y_1^F)^2 + (Y_2^A - Y_2^F)^2}}{\sqrt{(Y_1^A + Y_1^F)^2 + (Y_2^A + Y_2^F)^2}} \tag{3.2}$$

The effectiveness measure E can take any value between a maximum of unity and a minimum of zero. In a non-empty intersection between feasibility and admissibility, as portrayed in figure 3-1, we have $Y_1^A = Y_1^F$ and $Y_2^A = Y_2^F$ for all points in the CD intersection area and therefore $E = 1$. At the other extreme, for zero actual levels of output we have $Y_1^F = 0$, $Q_2^F = 0$ and

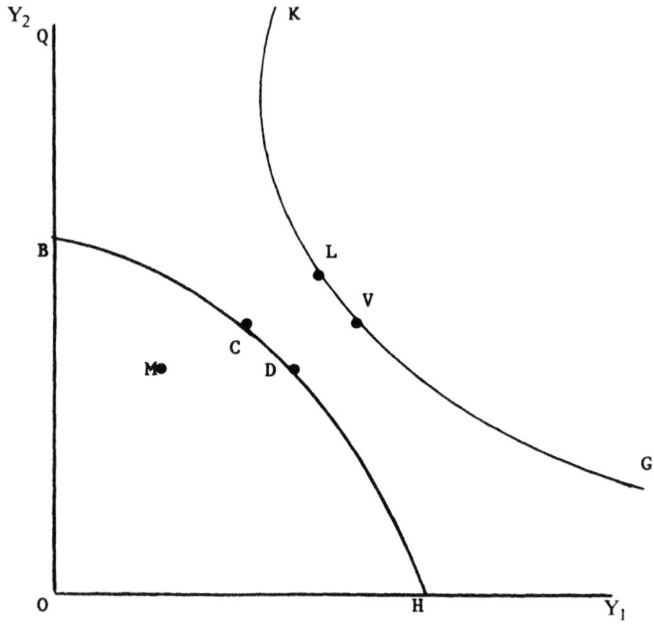

Figure 3-2. An Empty Feasible and Admissible Set.

consequently $E = 0$. The inbetween values of E indicate the extent to which the production of Y_1 and Y_2 is effective relative to profit and externality level objectives. A rational management will choose a combination of Y_1 and Y_2 which maximizes effectiveness. It is easy to see that such a combination must be on the efficiency frontier $\overline{BCDH}$.

Figure 3-2 illustrates graphically a case where the feasible set bounded by $\overline{BCDH}$ and the admissible set bounded by $\overline{KLVG}$ do not intersect. The effectiveness measure E will in this case be lower than unity. The maximum attainable effectiveness is equivalent to the distance between a feasible point D and an admissible point V which represent the minimum distance between the feasible and admissible set. The best solution under the circumstances is for the firm to produce the (Y_1^F, Y_2^F) combination indicated by D which simultaneously maximizes effectiveness and efficiency. Further increases in effectiveness beyond $\overline{DV}$ will require technological advances or relaxation in resource constraints which will push the feasibility constraint outward, or moderation of minimum admissible objectives which will push the admissibility boundary downward.

So far we assumed that the production function and therefore the efficiency frontier $\overline{BCDH}$ are known. In many cases only one actual point of the feasibility set (say point M in figure 3-2 is known. In general, this point may or may not be a maximum efficiency point. Suppose that point M is in fact within the feasibility set but not on the $\overline{BCDH}$ frontier due to wasteful (inefficient) production. In this case the effectiveness measure $\overline{ML}$ can be conceptually partitioned into an effectiveness component $\overline{CL}$ and a maximum feasible efficiency gain $\overline{MC}$. An optimal move will involve a movement from M to C to maximize technical efficiency or productivity, followed by a move along the efficiency frontier from C to D to maximize effectiveness. Of course, if the efficiency frontier is unknown, MC will be difficult, if not impossible, to estimate. The Charnes and Cooper model of relative efficiency (discussed in detail in chapter 8) may enable us under these circumstances to estimate a relative efficiency frontier for comparable operational units. If $\overline{BCDH}$ in figure 3-2 is a relative feasibility boundary then point M will register less than unity on the Cooper-Charnes efficiency scale. In this context, a movement from M to C which will improve relative efficiency to a maximum of unity can be undertaken. Subsequently to move from C to D will maximize effectiveness, given the *production* constraints.

Identification of Feasible and Admissible Sets

An effectiveness measure of less than unity indicates that the known feasible set and the admissible set do not intersect. In other words, a production solution which is both feasible and at the same time delivers managerial objectives of minimum acceptable profit and externality levels is unattainable. Management is faced with an empty solution space and the need to restructure its production or moderate its objectives. Increasing effectiveness can be attempted by upgrading productivity targets or settling for lower levels of profit and externality objectives. In this section we propose a simple algorithm designed to aid management (a) in identifying a feasible and admissible set (i.e., the intersection of sets A and F); and (b) in modifying minimal admissible objective levels to obtain a feasible and admissible set if the original one is empty.

The proposed algorithm is outlined in figure 3.3. This algorithm is designed to identify a feasible and admissible set of objectives. In the context of our previous example, we are looking for a set of profits and externality levels at time t, $\{\pi_t, Q_t\}$ that are technically feasible, and at the same time satisfy admissible profitability and externality levels. We assume, for the sake of simplicity, a two period model. The firm has no control over input

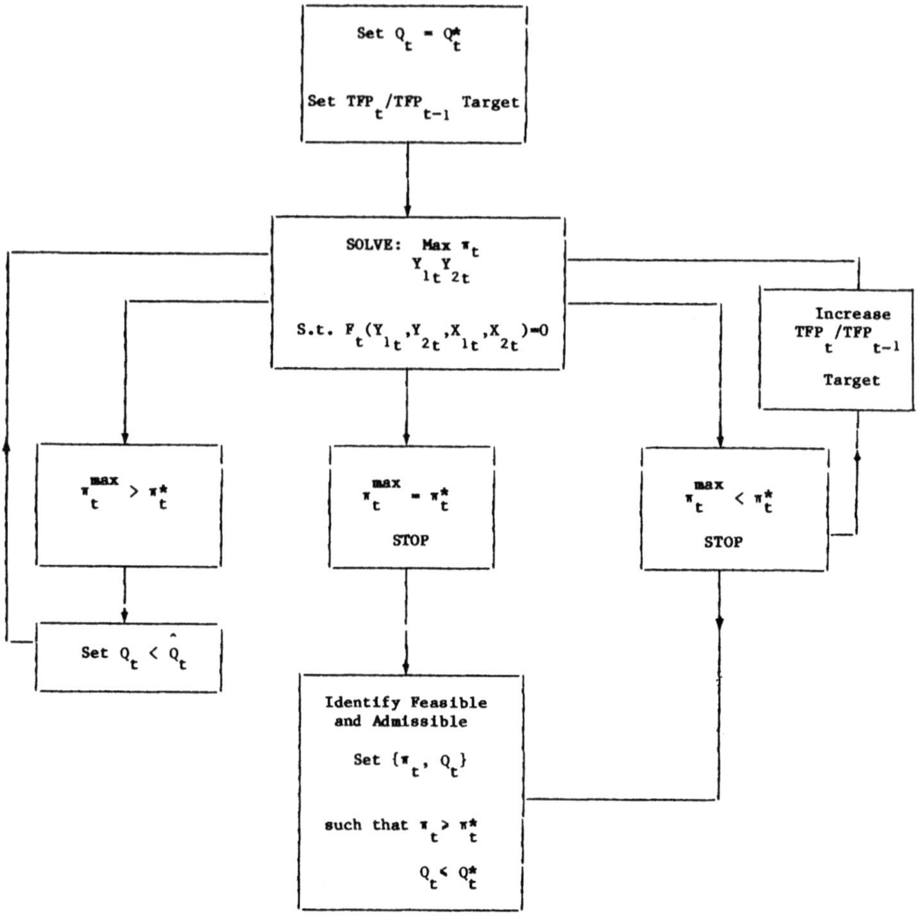

Figure 3-3. Algorithm for the Identification of Feasible and Admissible Set $\{\pi_t, Q_t: \pi_t \geq \pi_t^*; Q_t \leq Q_t^*\}$.

Source: Shakun and Sudit (1983).

and output prices. For period t management sets a minimum profit level π_t^*, a maximum externality level Q_t^*, and a productivity growth target $\text{TFP}_t/\text{TFP}_{t-1}$.

The starting point for the proposed algorithm is the maximum externality level $Q_t = Q_t^*$ and the productivity growth target $\text{TFP}_t/\text{TFP}_{t-1}$. These two goals determine the production function $F_t(Y_{1t}, Y_{2t}, X_{1t}, X_{2t})$. The SOLVE module in figure 3.3 is a standard Lagrange model which solves for the output levels of products 1 and 2, Y_{1t} and Y_{2t}, which maximize profits π_t subject to production and resource constraints. The maximum level of profits π_t^{max} obtained from SOLVE is compared with the minimum acceptable profit level π_t^*. If $\pi_\tau^{max} > \pi_t$, then the solution in SOLVE represents a feasible and admissible (π_t, Q_t) combination. We can subsequently try to identify an additional feasible and admissible (π_t, Q_t) pair by setting a new level of externality Q_t slightly lower than the maximum acceptable level Q_t^* and repeating the same sequence. This procedure is replicated as long as π_t^{max} for the newly selected level of Q_t is lower than π_t^*. Replication "stops" when either $\pi_t^{max} = \pi_t^*$ *or* $\pi_t^{max} < \pi_t^*$. At this point, we have identified a discrete feasible and admissible set consisting of feasible and acceptable profit and externality pairs. At the same time, we have also identified the set of output levels Y_{1t} and Y_{2t} of the two products that deliver feasible and admissible objectives.

If from the outset, we obtain via SOLVE $\pi_t^{max} < \pi_t^*$for $Q_t = Q_t^*$we know that the feasible and admissible set is empty. This follows from the simple observation that lowering the level of externality any further will increase costs and result in an even lower level of π_t^{max}. Obtaining a nonempty feasible and admissible set requires under these circumstances modification of productivity targets and resource constraints or relaxation of minimum profit requirements and maximum externality standards.

Suppose that application of the algorithm in figure 3.3 reveals an empty feasible and admissible set. The absence of any output combinations which satisfy feasible and acceptable objectives registers, in accordance with equation 3.2, an effectiveness level below unity ($E < 1$). One way to increase effectiveness is to revise upward the productivity improvement target TFP_t/TFP_{t-1}. If the higher productivity (technical change) target is attainable, then, upon implementation the technological (production function) constraint will be extended and the feasible boundary *BCDH* (figure 3-2) will be pushed outward, closer to the boundary KLVG of the admissible set. This shift in the feasible boundary represented by the production function $F_t(Y_{1t}, Y_{2t}, X_{1t}, X_{2t})$, will enable generation of (π_t, Q_t) solutions via the SOLVE module which will bring effectiveness closer to its maximum level of unity. Thus, the link between levels of efficiency (productivity) and effectiveness has been established in more concrete terms.

Within the framework of productivity-based management, it is possible to use algorithms of the type outlined in this section to determine the minimum level of productivity improvement necessary to obtain a maximum effectiveness level of unity (i.e., a nonempty feasible and admissible set). Such determination may be a desirable first step in the planning process. If the minimum necessary productivity improvement is perceived as attainable, strategies to assure its realization could be then designed on a priority basis, and modification of higher level objectives may be averted or postponed. Otherwise, a process of revising acceptable objective levels could begin before a crisis induced by low effectiveness levels materializes. Reassessment of higher level objectives may include downward revision of minimum acceptable levels of existing objectives and/or agreement on a new mix of existing and new objectives, similar to the referral process suggested by Shakun (1981).

The Importance of Joint Efficiency and Effectiveness Based Management

Our discussion in this chapter demonstrated that exclusive emphasis on efficiency (productivity) may, at times, impede effective management. For example, implementation of more efficient technologies or changing the mix of output to maximize TFP growth may succeed at the expense of a reduction in profitability or an increase of negative externalities. On the other hand, single minded preoccupation with effectiveness runs the danger of overlooking productivity-inducing strategies that may at times contribute considerably more to improvement in effectiveness than restructuring of financial or marketing policies. Hence, productivity-based management and effectiveness minded management supplement each other and ought to be pursued jointly.

Efficiency and effectiveness are related but clearly distinguishable concepts. Both can be rigorously defined and adequately measured. Purposeful organizations strive to attain acceptable levels of effectiveness in order to assure survival, continuity and growth. In a competitive world long term effectiveness can rarely be attained without efficiency oriented strategies and productivity control. Yet, sound productivity performance enhances effectiveness only if it is properly oriented toward higher level objectives. We have suggested in this chapter ways in which efficiency and effectiveness can be managerially linked to improve decision making, planning and control.

The examples used in the previous sections for illustration purposes related to a production of two products and a negative externality with a minimum acceptable level of profits and a maximum accepted externality level. However, the analytical and measurement techniques developed in this chapter can be generalized with only minor modifications. In essence, these methods of managing efficiency and effectiveness can be applied to any multi-purpose enterprise.

Notes

1. The discussion in this chapter is based in part on Shakun and Sudit (1983).
2. This measure of effectiveness was proposed by Melvin Shakun.

4 USE OF PRODUCTIVITY ACCOUNTING IN FINANCIAL ANALYSIS

Quantitative Standards as Productivity Targets

The use of quantitative standards is the most common manifestation of the application of productivity accounting to conventional cost accounting systems. Quantitative standards are specified in terms of desired ratios of input to output quantities. For example, a firm that employes L units of labor, and M units of materials to produce Y units of output would set quantitative standards of $\hat{L}/Y$ and $\hat{M}/Y$ for labor and materials respectively. $\hat{L}$ and $\hat{M}$ could be interpreted as the number of labor hours and the quantity of materials required to produce one unit of output. In other words, quantitative standards could be viewed as targets for input requirements (e.g., targets for quantities of inputs technically needed to produce one unit of output). The inverses of the quantitative standards ratios output per unit of labor, $\hat{Y}/L$ and output per unit of materials, $\hat{Y}/M$, are known respectively as partial labor productivity and materials productivity indexes. Obviously, many occupational categories of labor and types of materials are commonly used in the production process. Accordingly, numerous quantitative standards are designed as integral parts of conventional cost accounting systems. Along with the quantitative standards, price standards ($\hat{W}$ for labor and $\hat{V}$ for materials) are set as targets for the purchasing prices of labor and materials inputs. $\hat{W}$ is interpreted as the standard compensation paid to an hour of labor, and $\hat{V}$ is viewed as the standard price for which a unit of a certain material ought to be purchased.

Quantitative standards and price standards are essential features of standard costing systems practiced by most large and medium size manufacturing and technical enterprises as part of their management accounting systems. These standards are used as (a) guidelines for planning and decision making, and (b) yardsticks for performance. Ideally, the quantitative standards should be set at maximum attainable levels of technical efficiency (i.e., they should represent points on the production function or production frontier). In practice, the boundary of maximum attainable technical efficiency possibilities may not always be known. Consequently, quantitative standards are often set relative to past levels or external competitive market indicators of performance with some built-in improvement or stretch factors. Nonetheless, quantitative standards, regardless of how they are determined, are designed to function as a set of productivity targets. They are a collection of partial productivity indexes that serve as guidelines and yardsticks for maintaining, controlling and improving technical efficiency. Thus, any conventional standard costing contains, by the virtue of its design, some built-in components of a productivity-based management.

Productivity-Based Flexible Budgeting

Quantitative standards provide us with targets for quantities of inputs required to produce one unit of output. It is commonly assumed that these standards are valid for all relevant levels of production. That means that in the design and application of standard cost accounting we usually assume the prevalence of linear relationships throughout the relevant range of output. For example, if we set a quantitative standard of five hours of labor for the production of one widget, we would expect the use of 500,000 hours to produce 100,000 widgets and 750,000 hours to produce 150,000 widgets. If such linear relationships can serve as reasonable approximations for technically efficient input-output ratios over the relevant range of output, then total input requirements for any input can be simply obtained by multiplying the pertinent quantitative standard by the number of output units actually produced.

While the input-output linearity assumption is computationally convenient it should not be invoked if it does not constitute a reasonable approximation to efficient and attainable production relationships. Partial productivity indexes or input requirements per unit of output may at times change significantly with the level of production. Knowledge of the underlying production function would make it possible to set quantitative standard targets that are contingent on the level of output. It follows that, without loss of generality, we can specify the standard quantities of labor, $\hat{L}$, and the standard quantities of materials $\hat{M}$ as functions of the actual levels of output Y (i.e., $\hat{L} = \hat{L}(Y)$ and $\hat{M} = \hat{M}(Y)$).

The demand for the final product is likely to fluctuate. As a result, actual levels of output will change periodically. Flexible budgets are designed to accommodate frequent changes in output by making quantitative standards $\hat{L}(Y)$ and $\hat{M}(Y)$ contingent on actual levels of output. Static budgets, by contrast, set fixed quantitative standards for labor and materials predicated on one fixed target level of output. Flexible budgets are preferable to static budgets since they allow productivity targets to change with levels of actual outputs to reflect changes in efficient production possibilities as dictated by the underlying technology. Recognizing this important advantage, most companies use flexible budgeting techniques in their financial planning. Note that linear input-output relationships, while frequently assumed in practice, are not an essential feature of flexible budgeting. Any appropriate functional relationship between the required levels of inputs and actual outputs can be specified as long as these standard levels remain explicitly contingent on the actual level of output. Thus, flexible budgets incorporate schedules of productivity targets (i.e., quantitative standards) for all relevant levels of actual output.

Efficiency Variances as Indicators of Productivity Performance

Quantitative standards are designed to serve as guidelines, targets or yardsticks for actual productivity performance. Consequently, input quantities actually used to produce certain levels of output are periodically compared with predetermined standard levels of inputs deemed efficient for the levels of output actually produced. Deviations of actual inputs from target inputs are measured by efficiency variances. Suppose that L actual hours of labor and M actual units of materials are used to produce Y units of output. The predetermined quantitative standards for labor and materials required to produce Y are $\hat{L}(Y)$ and $\hat{M}(Y)$ respectively. The labor efficiency variance, LEV, and the materials efficiency variance MEV, are defined as follows:

$$LEV = (L - \hat{L}(Y))\hat{W} \tag{4.1}$$

and:

$$MEV = (M - \hat{M}(Y))\hat{V} \tag{4.2}$$

where $\hat{W}$ and $\hat{V}$ are respectively the predetermined standard prices for labor and materials.

The interpretation of efficiency variances is straightforward. For example, the labor efficiency variance LEV in (4.1) measures the labor costs incurred or saved as a result of the deviation of the actual labor hours from their predetermined output contingent standard quantity, assuming that the predetermined target for the compensation per hour, $\hat{W}$, is actually met. The materials efficiency variance, MEV, in (4.2) can be interpreted in an analogous manner. If actual hours L fall short of (exceed) standard hours $\hat{L}(Y)$ the unfavorable (favorable) labor efficiency variance indicates the labor costs incurred (saved) due to actual labor productivity performance being realized at levels lower (higher) than standard.

The efficiency variances in (4.1) and (4.2) are calculated on the assumption that inputs are purchased or hired at prices which equal predetermined standard prices. Since actual prices paid for the inputs are likely in general to deviate from targets, measures for these price variances have to be defined and monitored. Consequently, labor price variances, LPV, and materials price variance, MPV, are defined as follows:

$$LPV = L(W - \hat{W}) \tag{4.3}$$

and

$$MPV = M(V - \hat{V}) \tag{4.4}$$

where W and V are the actual prices for a unit of labor and a unit of materials respectively.

Price variances measure the effects on input costs of deviations of actual input prices from their targets. For example, a favorable (unfavorable) materials price variance, MPV, measures the materials costs saved (incurred) as a result of purchasing materials at a price lower (higher) than the predetermined standard price. The labor price variance, LPV, can be interpreted in an analogous manner.

For any input, the efficiency variance and the price variance add up to the flexible budget variance. Using the labor input as an example we obtain:

$$(L - \hat{L}(Y))\hat{W} + (W - \hat{W})L = WL - \hat{W}\hat{L}(Y)$$

Labor Efficiency Variance	+	Labor Price Variance	=	Flexible Budget Variance for Labor

The flexible budget variance for labor in (4.5) simply measures the deviation of actual labor costs, WL, from standard labor costs $\hat{W}\hat{L}(Y)$. The standard labor costs $\hat{W}\hat{L}(Y)$, are obtained by multiplying the standard number of hours $\hat{L}(Y)$, required to produce the actual level of output Y, by the standard compensation per hour $\hat{W}$. The flexible budget variance for materials could be defined in precisely the same manner as the one for labor in (4.5).

Thus, we see that the flexible budget variance for any direct input can be partitioned into its underlying efficiency and price variances. The efficiency variance is supposed to account for the portion of the flexible budget variance attributable to deviations of actual productivity performance from standard. The price variance is supposed to measure the effects on the flexible budget variance of deviations of actual input purchasing performance from standard.

Efficiency variances and price variances are routinely computed for all direct inputs by all companies that employ a standard costing system. These variances provide readily available tools for productivity-based cost and budget analysis. Efficiency variances indicating significant deviations can be further analyzed to identify major reasons for variations in productivity performance.

Interdependence among Variances and Evaluation of Productivity Performance

Detailed productivity analyses to identify factors contributing to large efficiency variances should be undertaken with a great deal of caution. The partitioning of the flexible budget variance in equation (4.5) to an efficiency variance and a price variance is technically correct. It does not follow however that efficiency variances unambiguously reflect deviations in productivity performance, or that price variances exclusively capture deviations in purchasing performance.

Possible patterns of interdependence between price and efficiency variances pose potential complications. The likelihood of such interdependence may increase if it is known or suspected that price and efficiency variances play a role in inducing managerial investigation and control measures which in turn implicitly or explicitly affect performance evaluation. For example, envision an organizational scenario under which the purchasing department is in charge of buying a certain material essential for the production process. If the purchasing people are interested in keeping materials' price variances favorable they may resort to buying lower quality materials at lower prices. Such practices may improve price variances readings at the expense of less favorable efficiency variances, since the production people will have to struggle to meet their productivity standards with lesser quality materials at their disposal. Obviously, in this case, a portion of the unfavorable efficiency variance should be attributed to deficient purchasing performance rather than to deficient productivity performance.

To continue with the same example, the production department may try to improve efficiency variance readings by insisting on unnecessarily high quality specifications for the materials they use. This use of excessively high quality materials (i.e., gold plating) may enable them to improve their productivity performance relative to predetermined standards at the expense of forcing the purchasing department to pay higher prices for materials. This chain of events will cause productivity performance to be overstated by the efficiency variance and purchasing performance to be understated by the price variance.

Strategic behavior of this type may be harmful to the company at large. Effort to transfer unfavorable variance from one department to another may not only obscure the meaning and interpretation of price and efficiency variances but may also result in less efficient operations and more costly production and purchasing.

Note that the interdependence between price and efficiency variances is not attributable solely to the failure to appropriately measure and specify levels of input quality. Suppose that the quality of materials is measured and specified in the quantitative standards. The purchasing department can try to improve its price variance readings by lengthening the search for materials. A longer search may result in contracting for purchases at lower prices. However, delays in purchasing and delivery of materials may strain the production process resulting in lower productivity. These types of problems occur mainly because numerous dimensions of performance are either not observable or are very costly to monitor. Attempts to attenuate strategic behavior by striving to specify, measure and set standards for all possible dimensions of performance (e.g., quality, time of delivery) may result in unduly restrictive guidelines and excessively costly audits.

The conventional definition of price variances in (4.3) and (4.4) creates a partial dependence of these measures on productivity performance. Price variances are computed by multiplying the *actual* quantity of the input by the difference between its actual and standard price. Yet it is productivity performance which affects the actual level of the input used. As a result, the price variance which is supposed to measure purchasing performance is also affected by productivity performance. The appropriate remedy for this type of interdependence is to measure purchasing performance by a modified price variance defined as the product of the *standard* input quantity and the difference between actual and standard input price. If this modified procedure is adopted, it should be remembered that the sum of the efficiency variance and the *modified* price variance is no longer equal to the flexible budget variance, as is the case in (4.5). Thus, the flexible budget variance for any input cannot be fully explained by productivity performance and purchasing performance.

A more important and potentially more troublesome type of interdependence is the one resulting from a functional relationship among the productivity performances of the various inputs. From standard production theory we know that partial productivity of one input depends on levels of most, if not all, other inputs in the production process. Consequently, all quantitative standards should be set jointly. Yet even if this is done, unfavorable or favorable variances of one input can result, in large part from better or worse than standard productivity performance in other inputs. This complicates the role of efficiency variances as indicators of efficient performance.

The Role of Indirect Inputs and Capital in Productivity Accounting

In conventional standard cost accounting systems quantitative standards and efficiency variances are computed and analyzed for direct inputs only. Inputs are considered direct if they can be related technically to the volume of output produced. By contrast, indirect inputs are conceptualized as resources whose contribution to the level of production can be traced or understood in a roundabout manner. For example, hours worked by people in line jobs in production can be technically associated with the quantity of output. Hours worked by corporate staff, given the usual state of knowledge of the production process, can be only indirectly related to the quantity of output. Consequently, the former labor input is classified as direct, while the latter labor input is usually considered an indirect input. In most management accounting systems only categories of labor and materials, the quantities of which can be technically or engineeringly related to quantities of outputs, are classified as direct. All other resources employed are viewed as indirect.

How does this accounting approach to input-output relationships differ from the economic view of the production process? Conventional microeconomic analysis assumes that the total production process of the firm can be completely defined by the production function $Y = f(X_1, X_2, X_i, \ldots, X_n)$, where all n inputs used by the firm can be technically associated with the volume of output Y. The i-th input X_i can be a capital input, technology input or any other resource used by the firm to produce its output. Appropriate specification of the economic production function requires perfect knowledge of the production process. Specifically, we have to know the precise contribution of each resource or input to output, and how these contributions vary with changes in the combinations of the inputs. Furthermore, the economic production function is supposed to encompass short-term relationships between inputs and output under circumstances where some inputs are fixed, as well as input-output relationships within time spans long enough to allow for changes in all inputs (i.e., when all inputs are variable). Thus, the economic production function, to the extent that it is estimable, allows for partial average productivity measures (e.g., Y/X_i for the i-th input) for all inputs. It also makes possible the computation of marginal productivities (e.g., $\partial Y/\partial X_i$ for the i-th input). Both average and marginal productivities of any particular input can be stated as functions of all other inputs, reflecting the productivity interdependence among inputs. Knowledge of the economic production function thus affords intelligent determination of quantitative standards for all inputs, as well as the use of efficiency variances to measure actual productivity performance vis-à-vis standard for all resources involved in the production process.

Standard cost accounting systems have to come to terms with reality. Under most circumstances, much of the information required for a complete specification of the economic production function is either tenuous or unavailable. Under these conditions it is reasoned that only a subset of inputs (e.g., direct labor and direct materials) can be intelligently related to the volume of output. For all other inputs, indirect and overhead, our knowledge and information simply do not permit a meaningful estimation of their input-output relationships. In view of our imperfect knowledge of the production process, the best cost performance analysis which could be undertaken for indirect costs or overhead inevitably requires selection of somewhat arbitrary cost allocation schemes. As a result, the standards used for indirect costs are mostly predetermined allocation rates (i.e., budgeted indirect cost per units of activity) based on past experience. However, normally no distinct quantitative standards or input requirement targets are set for indirect input. In other words, cost accountants budget for various categories of indirect cost but do *not*, as a rule, set productivity targets and input price standards for indirect inputs.

Productivity-based budgeting in cost accounting is thus confined to a subset of direct inputs, chiefly direct labor and materials. One of the most troublesome aspects of this approach is that capital inputs are not considered direct inputs and are therefore excluded from the conventional productivity-based budgeting analysis. The treatment of capital inputs as indirect is generally not due to lack of information, but is inherent in traditional accounting methodology.

Capital related flows appear in the management accounting framework mainly in the form of depreciation expenses and interest payments, both viewed as indirect costs. In manufacturing companies depreciation expenses are commonly classified as indirect factory overhead. Since depreciation is not perceived as exclusively related to the volume of output, no input-output (productivity) targets are specified for capital.

From an economic-engineering viewpoint capital inputs are direct inputs into the production process. All produced tools of production (e.g., plant, machinery, equipment tools etc.) are defined as capital. These productive assets are instrumental in the production of output by providing flows of services (inputs). For example, machines, when utilized in production, provide flows of machine hours in much the same way that employees provide their skills and talents in the form of person-hours. Consequently, if labor hours and materials are direct inputs in the sense that they can be technically related to volume of output, then machine hours and tool hours qualify by the same logic as direct capital inputs.

Productivity accounting should therefore be broadened to include measurement and analysis of capital productivity. Quantitative standards for various types of machine hours per unit of output, tool hours per unit of output, and equipment hours per unit of output ought to be determined so that actual capital to output ratios could be periodically measured and compared to standards.

Capital efficiency variances analogous to labor efficiency variances and materials efficiency variances can be computed to measure deviations of actual capital productivity performance from standards. For example, denote K as the actual level of machine hours and $\hat{K}(Y)$ as the standard quantity of machine hours required to produce Y units of output. The capital efficiency variance KEV can be defined as:

$$KEV = (K - \hat{K}(Y))\hat{r} \tag{4.6}$$

where $\hat{r}$ is the standard cost per machine hour.

The standard cost of a machine hour can be estimated as follows. Suppose that the average market price of the machine throughout the year is estimated at \$1,200,000. The target annual cost of capital for the firm is 10%. The use of the machine in the production process during the year ties up \$1,200,000 in funds, the opportunity costs of which have \$1,200,000 × (.10) = \$120,000. Suppose that the quantitative standard for machine capital specifies that two machine hours are required to produce one unit of output. If 30,000 units of the final product are actually produced during the year, then the standard quantity of capital required to produce this quantity is 60,000 machine hours. Consequently, the standard cost of a machine hour can be set at $\hat{r} = \$120{,}000/60{,}000 = \$2$.

If 70,000 machine hours were actually used to produce 30,000 units of output, the efficiency variance for the machine in question can be computed as: $KEC = (70{,}000 - 60{,}000)2 = \$20{,}000$. Thus, the firm incurred \$20,000 in additional capital costs as a result of the actual productivity of the machine falling below the productivity standard or target.

Determination of Efficient and Effective Quantitative Standards under Uncertainty

In the real world quantitative standards have to be set in the face of demand uncertainty. Usually these standards are predetermined in the sense that they are set, ex-ante, before the actual quantity demanded of the final product is known. On a superficial level of analysis, it may appear that the flexible budget framework is well suited to handle this type of uncertainty since flexible quantitative standards are contingent on the level of output. Unfortunately, straightforward application of conventional flexible budgeting procedures do not, in general, guarantee that adherence to quantitative standards will result in efficient and effective production decisions.

To illustrate this point, consider a production of output Y by capital, K, and labor L. The production function is $Y = f(K, L)$, and the demand function for the final product is $Y = Y(P, U)$, where P is the price for a unit of output and U is a random disturbance term. Thus, the demand for the final product Y is uncertain. Price of labor and capital, w and r respectively, are uncertain as well. In a decentralized setting, top management normally sets all quantitative standards for the production department ex-ante (i.e., before the uncertainties concerning quantity demanded and input prices are resolved). Suppose, for the sake of simplicity, that the firm pursues a single objective of profit maximization. In this case, if top management sets profit maximizing quantitative standards for labor and capital (i.e., standards which maximize *expected* profits), then, adherence to such standards will bring about efficient as well as effective production. Profit maximization guarantees by definition, in this single objective example, the attainment of maximum effectiveness. Maximum efficiency (i.e., producing on the efficiency frontier $Y = f(K, L)$ is of course a necessary condition for profit maximization.

Determination of profit maximizing quantitative standards in the face of demand and input price uncertainty is not a simple matter. In setting those standards *ex-ante* top management must anticipate the type of adjustments in production it can implement *ex-post* (i.e., after quantity demanded and input prices become known). Normally, it should be possible to adjust the levels of some inputs within a short span of time after uncertainty is resolved, while other inputs will not lend themselves to change in the short term. The former are commonly termed variable inputs, while the latter are usually designated as fixed inputs. In the context of our example, suppose that labor is a variable input and capital is a fixed input. It is plausible to assume that the quantity of hours worked can be rapidly adjusted, via hiring lay-offs and overtime, once demand and input prices are known. On the other hand, adjusting the quantity of plant and equipment may require a considerably longer period of time. Thus, the level of capital determined ex-ante can be treated for all practical purposes as fixed ex-post, because it is likely that by the time capital can be adjusted, demand and input prices will be subject to further uncertain changes.

Keeping these considerations in mind, top management must allow for the probabilities of ex-post adjustments if it is to maximize the expected profits of the firm. We must remember however that ex-post adjustment in the variable labor input will be made in an environment where the predetermined level of capital is fixed at $K = \bar{K}$ (The bar denotes a fixed level of capital input). With fixed capital, the relevant production function for ex-post labor adjustments is the short term production function, $Y = g(K, \bar{L})$, not the long term production function $Y = f(K, L)$. Changes in labor will be subject to decreasing marginal productivity (diminishing returns) due to the fixed amount of capital that labor will have to work with. As a result, in maximizing expected profits, the optimal level of capital is determined ex-ante using the long term production function, while simultaneously taking into account that ex-post adjustments in labor would entail movements along a short-term production function. Hartman (1976) develops in detail the optimal (profit maximizing) input decisions under these circumstances.

The various implications of the foregoing considerations on the determination of profit maximizing quantitative standards have been discussed in detail by Itami (1975), Ijiri and Itami (1973) and Ravid and Sudit (1983). Profit maximizing quantitative standards are set on the basis of optimal (profit maximizing) input and output quantities. For example, if the output and input level solutions for maximization of expected profits are Y^*, K^* and L^* then the profit maximizing quantitative standards are K^*/Y^* and L^*/Y^*. The problem is that, in allowing for ex-post adjustments, these optimal quantitative standards depend not only on ex-ante expected quantity demanded and input prices, but also on ex-post actually realized demand and input prices. Since ex-post actual levels are not known in advance, definite profit maximizing quantitative standards cannot be set ex-ante! At best, only *formulae* for optimal quantitative standards *contingent* on ex-post demand and input price information can be determined ex-ante. These formulae will have to be continuously revised as more information flows with the profit maximizing standards finally determined only when all uncertainties are resolved. In the context of our example, the optimal level of capital $K^* = \bar{K}$ has to be determined ex-ante with the view that the optimal quantities of labor and output, L^* and Y^* respectively, would be finally determined only after the quantity demanded for the final product and input prices become known. In this manner the necessary ex-post profit maximizing adjustments in hours worked and the number of units produced can be made, as the production department attempts to meet those standards. Consequently, if definite quantitative standards, based only on ex-ante expectations, are set in advance then they are unlikely to be profit maximizing. Adherence to such inappropriate standards of productivity performance is unlikely to be effective since it will almost surely bring about deviations from the maximum attainable level of profits. These shortfalls in effectiveness will be caused by inefficient production (i.e., failure to adjust variable inputs and output along a short term production function).

The correct procedure for the determination of profit maximizing quantitative standards under uncertainty differs from the conventional flexible budget design. This procedure is outlined in detail by Ravid and Sudit (1983) and calls for the following steps: (a) Ex-ante, set the level of the fixed inputs (e.g., the quantity of capital, $K^* = \bar{K}$), so as to maximize expected profits with full allowance for ex-post profit maximizing adjustments in variable inputs (e.g., the quantity of labor, L); (b) Ex-post, when information about quantity demand for the final product and input prices become known, set the profit-maximizing quantitative standards (e.g., L^*/Y^* and $\bar{K}/Y^*$) based on the optimal quantities of the variable inputs (e.g., $L = L^*$) and output (e.g., $Y = Y^*$). Thus, only the quantitative standards for the fixed inputs (e.g., $K = K^* = \bar{K}$) are communicated by top management to the production department in the course of the budgeting process. Quantitative standards for the variable inputs (e.g., $L = L^*$) and outputs (e.g., $Y = Y^*$) are communicated ex-post. The production department guided by these ex-post standards has enough time to adjust the quantities of variable inputs and the level of production to assure profit maximization.

Under this recommended budgeting procedure, profit maximizing quantitative standards are communicated only when all relevant information for their *timely* implementation is available. Standard quantities for fixed inputs have to be set ex-ante despite lack of complete information. Otherwise, they will become unattainable before the circumstances upon which they are predicated change. Quantitative standards for variable inputs can be optimally provided when all relevant information is secured without affecting attainability of these targets. Consequently, setting such targets prematurely is likely to reduce effectiveness. Obviously, if different inputs require different time spans for adjustment, then the procedure for setting profit maximizing standards for these inputs should be modified accordingly. The underlying principle is to set quantitative standards based on the best available information subject to the time dimension of attainability. The flexible budgeting system under uncertainty ought to be based on productivity targets that are contingent on demand and input prices. The resulting profit maximizing input standards are likely to be nonlinear functions of output due to the prevalence of diminishing returns in ex-post adjustments.

5 TFP-BASED FINANCIAL ANALYSIS

TFP-Based Financial Analysis and Flexible Budgeting

The common feature of the TFP-based financial analysis techniques proposed in this section is their reliance on the total factor productivity index as an aggregate productivity performance indicator. TFP growth targets implicit in budgets can be computed ex-ante, and actual TFP gains underlying actual financial performance can be calculated ex-post for use in audits, performance evaluation, and as a basis for corrective actions.

In our discussion of the use of productivity accounting in financial analysis (see chapter 4), we argued that productivity based financial analysis is already practiced by many companies through their use of conventional flexible budgeting and standard costing systems. It is therefore appropriate to ask whether there is any value added in supplementing analysis of quantitative standards and efficiency variances with TFP-based techniques.

The use of quantitative standards provides us with numerous partial productivity standards, which can be compared with actual performance. However, as pointed in our discussion in chapter 4, those partial productivities are likely to be interdependent. A partial productivity of one input is likely to depend on levels of other inputs used in the production process. We know that the TFP index is a weighted average of all partial productivity index. Total factor productivity performance reflects therefore the net effects of all the partial productivity performances inclusive of their interdependencies. It is an aggregate indicator of the overall physical efficiency in the use of resources. Consequently, the TFP is a productivity equivalent of the bottom line. We shall demonstrate in this chapter that the use of total factor productivity in financial analysis, along with other aggregate indicators of performance, supplements flexible budgeting by providing us with additional insights, analytical tools and efficient short-cuts in productivity based budgeting, auditing and financial planning. To facilitate the illustration of TFP-based financial analysis techniques and their uses we provide in the section below a detailed actual case study example of this type of analysis.

A Case Study of TFP-Based Financial Analysis (Eldor and Sudit (1981))

The numerical example of TFP-based financial analysis presented in this section follows strictly the discussion by Eldor and Sudit (1981 pp. 608–611), with only minor modifications and extensions. It is based on an actual procedure adopted by a major U.S. corporation. The data was modified to preserve anonymity.

In this particular case study a Laspeyres TFP index was used for computational convenience. Subsequent sensitivity analysis showed that, for all practical purposes, the numerical differences between the Laspeyres formula and the Tornquist type of approximation to a Divisia index were slight.

To construct the Laspeyres TFP index, price indexes for the various outputs of the case study corporation were computed. The revenues generated by each output were then separately adjusted for their specific price changes through deflation by their respective Laspeyres price indexes. Similar procedures were applied to the inputs. Employment compensations for various categories of employment were repriced at base year compensation rates via deflation by their respective Laspeyres employment compensation indexes (reflecting changes in wages and fringe benefits). Each individual capital equipment account was repriced at base year prices, according to engineering estimates of the age distribution of surviving plant, by applying the appropriate capital plant price indexes. Consequently, all capital inputs were stated in terms of replacement costs at base year prices. Likewise, materials, rents and services purchased by the corporation from outside suppliers were deflated by appropriate price indexes. The sum of all inputs in constant (base year) dollars for a certain year served as a proxy for the quantity of total inputs in that particular period.

Table 5-1 presents data derived from conventional income statements for three consecutive years: year zero (our base-year for the purpose of productivity computation), year one and year two. Net income has declined in year one as compared to year zero by four million, and has increased in year two over year one by $209 million. For the sake of brevity, inputs and outputs are presented in an aggregated form. The subcomponents were also aggregated via the use of the Laspeyres formula.

A conventional financial analysis of the dismal performance in year one and the strong recovery of year two would center on the relative change in revenues versus expenses, based largely on income statement data. Good management performance could be implied by year two data, while less than satisfactory performance could be inferred from year one results. These implications, of course, could lead to incomplete or even erroneous

Table 5-1. Conventional Accounting Data, $ Millions (Source: Profit and Loss Statements)

	Year O base year (1)	*Year 1 (2)*	*Change Year 1 −Year 0 (3) =(2)−(1)*	*Year 2 (4)*	*Change Year 2 −Year 1 (5) =(4)−(2)*
(1) Revenues	7,903	8,742	839	9,904	1,162
Expenses					
(2) Total labor expenses	2,953	3,334	381	3,711	377
(3) Materials, rents and services	1,121	1241	120	1445	204
(4) Depreciation expense	1,105	1224	119	1342	118
(5) All non-income taxes	597	655	58	727	72
(6) Total operating expenses	5776	6454	678	7225	771
(7) Taxes and other financial factors	1156	1321	165	1503	182
(8) Net income lines (1)−(6)−(7)	971	967	(4)	1,176	209
(9) Capital return in base-year lines (7) + (8)	2,127	—	—	—	—

Source: Eldor and Sudit (1981), p. 609.

Table 5-2. Computation of Productivity Gain Base-Year $ (Millions)

	Year 0 (base-year) (1)	*Year 1 (2)*	*Year 2 (3)*
Outputs			
(1) Total operating revenues	7,903	8,326	8,951
(2) All non-income taxes	597	621	647
(3) Materials, rents and services	1,121	1,135	1,254
(4) Depreciation	1,105	1,116	1,146
(5) Total net output lines (1) − (2) − (3) − (4)	5,080	5,454	5,904
Inputs			
(6) Labor input	2,953	3,942	2,906
(7) Average net capital base	28,134	28,481	29,434
(8) Base-year rate of return (Table 1 line 9) ÷ (Table 2 line 7)	7.756%	7.756%	7.756%
(9) Capital input line (7) × line (8)	2,127	2,209	2,283
(10) Total *inputs* lines (6) + (9)	5,080	5,151	5,189
(11) *Productivity gain* lines (5) − (10)	−0−	303	715
(12) Productivity index	100.0	105.9	113.8

Source: Eldor and Sudit (1981), p. 609.

conclusions. Management could have done a good job of improving efficiency and cutting cost in year one, but were still not able to overcome the inflationary rise in expenses, thus suffering a decline in net income. Year two, on the other hand, could have witnessed sloppy management practices, but a very rapid rise in the price of output (due to completely exogenous factors) could have masked management inefficiency and improved net income.

Clearly a greater insight into the specific contribution of management to net income bottom line performance is desirable. This can be achieved by separating operating factors, over which management has greater leverage, from price factors related to exogenous inflationary factors. The price quantity separation facilitates a detailed comparison of actual results with quantitative standards and price standards set in a flexible budget framework, as shown in chapter 4. Our purpose here is to illustrate an alternative analytical framework predicated on the computation and analysis of the TFP changes implicit in the financial results.

In table 5-2 all price factors are netted out and revenues and expenses are converted to physical output and inputs, expressed in base year dollars. The excess of outputs' increase over inputs is total factor productivity gain. In year one productivity gain amounted to $303 million, or 5.9% increase over year zero. In year two productivity gain was $715 million over year zero, or $412 million net annual gain for that year.

The difference between current dollar data and constant, base year dollar data constitutes the effect of price changes, or inflationary impact. That impact is presented in table 5-3 for each of the relevant output and input components.

Table 5-4 presents the concluding analysis of the factors affecting change in net income, expressed in meaningful categories. During year one, the inability to sufficiently raise the prices of output to offset the inflationary rise in the prices of inputs resulted in a net negative inflationary impact of $224 million. This, together with the increase in tax and financial expenses, was not sufficiently offset by the rise in productivity, finally resulting in a decline of net income of four million.

During year two, management has increased productivity gain significantly to $412 million. This gain, together with a much larger increase in the price of output, nearly offsetting the inflationary increase in expenses, resulted in a final increase in net income of 209 million.

Both table 5-1 and table 5-4 have the same bottom line, but is should by now be apparent to the reader that the analysis introduced here and portrayed by table 5-4 contains information which is relevant to the evaluation of management performance.

Distribution of Productivity Gains

An analysis of the distribution of productivity gains often provides a useful way to evaluate the effects of productivity growth on financial performance. The case study computations in the section above illustrated how TFP gains can be translated from an index reading to a dollar equivalent. The productivity gain in year one (table 5-4) can be interpreted as providing $303 millions in funds generated by the increased efficiency in operations. In the absence of such productivity gains, an additional $303 millions would have had to be raised by increasing prices (demand conditions permitting) or by additional investment (i.e., increasing capital inputs). Otherwise, payments to the factors of production (i.e., owners, employees and supplies) would have had to be reduced.

Consider a scenario under which savings on payments to outside suppliers for materials, rents and services, as well as tax payments are beyond the control of management. Furthermore, assume that demand elasticities for the

Table 5-3. Impact of Inflation, $(Millions)

	Current$ Col(2) Table 1	*Price effects Year 1 – Year 0 Col(1) – Col(2) Table 2*	*Current$ Col(4) Table 1*	*Price effects Year 2 – Year 0 Col(3) – Col(3) Table 2*	*Price effects Year 2 – Year 1 Col(4) – Col(2)*
(1) Revenues	8,742	416	9,904	953	537
(2) Materials, rents and services	1,241	106	1,445	191	85
(3) All non-income Taxes	655	34	727	80	46
(4) Labor expenses	3,334	392	3,711	805	413
(5) Depreciation	1,224	108	1,342	196	88

Source: Eldor and Sudit (1981), p. 610.

Table 5-4. Factors Affecting Change in Net Income, $(Millions)

	Increase (+)	*Decrease (−)*	*Increase (+)*	*Decrease (−)*
Operating factors				
(1) Productivity gain (Annual)	303		412	
(2) Capital input increase	82		74	
(3) Total operating factors	385		486	
Inflationary factors				
(4) Output (Sales) prices	416		537	
(5) Materials, rents and services		106		85
(6) All non-income taxes		34		46
(7) Labor		392		413
(8) Depreciation		108		88
(9) Total inflationary factors		224		95
(10) Total tax and financial factors		165		182
(11) Change in net income		4	209	

Source: Eldor and Sudit (1981) p. 610.

products and services produced are such that additional revenues cannot be raised simply by raising prices. In this case, in the absence of any productivity gains the firm would have to reduce returns to owners (i.e., net income) and/or compensation to employees.

Normally, the firm has at least some degree of discretion over the distribution of productivity gains to (a) its customers via pricing; (b) its employees via compensation, and (c) its owners via dividends and retained earnings. Decisions concerning such distributions are usually taken as part of the management of the sources and uses of funds. In our case study (table 5-4) productivity gains constitute only one of three sources of funds. Additional funds were raised through price increases ($416 millions) and capital input increases ($82 millions). thus, the specific distribution of productivity gains cannot be meaningfully isolated. However, as statement of the sources and uses of funds, table 5-4's innovative feature is the explicit allowance for the financial impact of growth in productivity.

The same principles that are applied to ex-post (after-the-fact) TFP-based financial analysis can be applied to budgeting. The emphasis merely shifts to forward looking financial planning. Suppose that the data in table 5-1 represents a *budgeted* income statement for future years one and two (year zero is the current period). Table 5-2 becomes a *budgeted* productivity statement. All the specific price indexes used to deflate nominal inputs and outputs to obtain real inputs and outputs are projected as estimates of future changes in those prices. Table 5-3 becomes a statement of budgeted effects of inflation. Table 5-4 assumes the role of a productivity based statement of budgeted sources and uses of funds.

TFP-based budgeting broadens the budget framework by explicitly budgeting for changes in total factor productivity. Conventional flexible budgeting procedures budget productivity gains by specifying targeted changes in quantitative standards (see chapter 4 for a detailed discussion). These two approaches to productivity based budgeting are by no means mutually exclusive. In fact, they complement each other well. Setting productivity standards through specification of numerous quantitative standards allows for a detailed budgeting of input requirements. Budgeting for projected changes in total factor productivity provides us with a measure of overall projected changes in the efficiency of the use of resources. The TFP is a less detailed measure of productivity performance when examined as a single index number. However, the TFP index can be shown to be a weighted sum of the partial productivity indexes which are the inverse ratios of the quantitative standards. As a result, the TFP as a measure of overall productivity performance does not lend itself to many potentially distortive effects of the interdependence among partial productivity indexes.

Productivity Based Budget Audits

Total factor productivity targets can be useful in supplementing quantitative standards in a productivity based budgeting process. This same analytical framework which is used ex-ante for financial planning can be applied ex-post for auditing. Within the framework of a TFP-based budget audit, actual partial productivity indexes are compared with their respective predetermined quantitative standards and actual TFP performance is compared with TFP budgeted targets. Significant variances in actual productivity performance versus budgeted yardsticks can be identified for further investigation. Subsequent analysis can assess the effects of these deviations in productivity performance on the financial performance of the enterprise and explore the causes for such variances.

TFP variances can be simply measured as differences between actual levels of the TFP_t at time t and target levels, $\hat{TFP}_t$, or as differences between actual changes in TFP from time t to time $t + 1$, TFP_{t+1}/TFP_t, and budgeted targets for TFP change (TFP_{t+1}/TFP_t). The problems associated with the development of TFP targets or yardsticks require further elaboration.

Technologically based absolute total factor productivity standards are difficult to establish since TFP represents an overall measure of physical efficiency rather than the productivity of a specific, engineeringly well-defined process. Consequently, relative TFP standards, such as improvement over past productivity performance, over performance of competitors or producers in related industries, are often selected as practical and reasonable targets. In analyzing budgeted TFP performance relative to standards, several considerations should be borne in mind: (a) TFP is quite sensitive to business cycles; (b) Not all factors affecting productivity performance are under management control; (c) Technological innovations may temporarily retard productivity growth in return for improved future performance; (d) TFP readings can be improved temporarily at the expense of quality of products or services.

Total factor productivity analysis can play an important role in a budget audit. Suppose that some actual levels of partial productivity indexes fall significantly below this respective quantitative standard while others exceed their respective target. As a result, analysis of the variances will indicate unfavorable efficiency variances for some inputs and favorable for others. The TFP variance will show the net effect of these offsetting deviations in partial productivities on overall efficiency performance relative to target. For example, if the actual TFP performance is close to target then we may conclude that overall productivity performance was satisfactory. The deviations in the efficiency variances may be attributable to substitution effects among the inputs reflecting changes in the structure of production. If this hypothesis is confirmed upon further investigation, then corrective action in this case may be mostly oriented toward revising quantitative standards to reflect the changing structure of production.

Selective Sequential Budgetary Audit Based on Total Factor Productivity Indicators (Ishikawa and Sudit (1981))

Frequent resort to a comprehensive budgetary auditing and analysis may prove costly in terms of (a) explicit transaction costs; (b) implicit opportunity costs of managerial time spent; and (c) increased observed and unobserved organizational frictions. If such costs are significant and need to be attenuated, a less frequent exercise of full-fledged audit may be called for. For example, partial audits may be undertaken quarterly, while comprehensive audits may be undertaken yearly or whenever serious performance problems are indicated.

We proceed in this section to propose a method of selective sequential budgetary audit designed to reduce the frequency of comprehensive audits, while maintaining effective control over actual performance vs. standards. To that end, we propose that certain performance indicators be initially examined to determine the type of audit required. The approach suggested here corresponds with some minor modifications to the procedure developed by Ishikawa and Sudit (1981) concerning a sequential zero based budgeting procedure.[1]

Consider the following aggregate performance indicators:

1. Profitability—levels and rates of change in actual earnings vs. standards.
2. Growth—rates of change in total operating revenues (actual vs. standards).
3. Productivity—Actual total factor productivity levels and rates of change vs. standards.

In the planning process management determines satisfactory earnings, market shares and growth rates and translates these general performance objectives to price standards, quantitative standards and TFP standards. However, the process of monitoring each period numerous specific budget variances and the subsequent investigation of all significant deviations can be costly and time consuming. We therefore propose that a periodic budget audit start with preliminary examination of the aggregate performance indicators of profitability, growth and productivity. Subsequent scope and detail of audit procedures should depend on an initial reading of these indicators.

If significant deviations are observed in profitability indicators only, with satisfactory recordings for growth and productivity, specific audits of input unit price performance follow first. The rationale behind this inference is straightforward. As long as TFP indexes indicate satisfactory performance levels, it is likely that there are no significant problems with input quantities X or output variables Y. Satisfactory growth indicators increase the likelihood that output price performance P is satisfactory. Thus, by process of elimination it is probable that adequate corrective action can be indicated as a result of a thorough audit of input price performance only.

By the same logic, deviations in growth indicators only, establishes the priority for specific audit of output prices P. Derivations in total factor productivity indexes will point to the priority of specific audits of input quantity performance (i.e., of deviations of budgeted input quantities from standards).

Simultaneous deviations in any two indicators will indicate lower priority for auditing the variables underlying the third satisfactory index. In some cases, partial auditing may adequately identify causes of deviations in the variables underlying the two unsatisfactory indexes, eliminating the need to examine the variables underlying the satisfactory indicator.

If all three indicators register unsatisfactory variations, a full-fledged audit may be required. However, even in this case it may be preferable to proceed sequentially, starting the audit procedure with analysis of the variables underlying the most unfavorable performance indicator. This type of sequential approach is likely to identify the most crucial problem areas earlier, thereby expediting efficient corrective measures.

The alternative paths of the sequential procedure are outlined schematically in 5-5.[2] In cases (1), (2), and (3), when a single indicator at a time gives nonsatisfactory readings, movement from the first phase to the next phase of the analysis is required only if the first stage of the analysis failed to adequately identify problems and prescribed corrective actions. Otherwise, analysis terminates and the option of foregoing a full fledged audit may be contemplated. Managerial determination of what constitutes "failure of analysis" at any phase is inevitably judgmental and depends among other things on the perception of the severity of consequences of various degrees of shortfalls in performance. These perceptions are likely to be subjective and case specific.

In cases when two or all three indicators simultaneously produce nonsatisfactory signals the procedure calls for starting with the most nonsatisfactory indicator, as if this indicator was the only one showing negative readings, and proceeding with the analytical phases in (1), (2), or (3). If there is a "failure of partial analysis" extension to a comprehensive budget, audit may follow.

We believe that our sequential procedure is *likely* to provide the budget analyst with the option of carrying out selective and partial audits with prospects for potentially good results. This important feature of our TFP-based sequential approach requires some additional qualifications. By a partial budget audit we mean an audit of a subset of all quantity and price variables (e.g., input quantities only). Before applying the selected sequential auditing procedure, we should assess dependence among all input and output budget variables (prices as well as quantities) in the overall organizational process. To the extent that the latter interdependence is strong, a partial analysis of subcomponents may, at times, miss the point. Interdependence therefore introduces an element of uncertainty into the partial procedure in

Table 5-5. Outline of Selective Sequential Productivity-Base Zero-Base Budgeting Analysis

	Monitored Indicators	*Reading of Indicators*	*Sequence of Budget Audit*
(1)	TFP $\tilde{Y}/\tilde{X}$ GROWTH $R = PY'$ PROFITABILITY w_k	Nonsatisfactory Satisfactory Satisfactory	Analyze: First: Output Y Next: Inputs X vs $\hat{X}(Y)$
(2)	TFP $\tilde{Y}/\tilde{X}$ GROWTH $R = PY'$ PROFITABILITY w_k	Satisfactory Nonsatisfactory Satisfactory	Analyze: First: Prices P Next: Output Y
(3)	TFP $\tilde{Y}/\tilde{X}$ GROWTH $P = PY'$ PROFITABILITY w_k	Satisfactory Satisfactory Nonsatisfactory	Analyze: First: Unit Cost W vs $\hat{W}$ Next: Inputs X vs $X(\hat{Y})$
	TFP $\tilde{Y}/\tilde{X}$ GROWTH $R = PY'$ PROFITABILITY w_k	Any two out of three indicators Nonsatisfactory	Analyze: A single indicator with highest deviation first (in accordance with above procedure) (1), (2), or (3)
	TFP $\tilde{X}/\tilde{X}$ GROWTH $R = PY'$ PROFITABILITY w_k	All three indicators Nonsatisfactory	Analyze: Indicator with higher deviation first. Second highest Next according to (1), (2), or (3) or resort to conventional zero-base budgeting.

the sense that causes for variances may be overlooked or misdiagnosed. The tradeoff is between a potentially more accurate comprehensive budget audit and a faster and less costly partial audit.

In consequence, the budgeting procedure proposed in this section is *sequential* in the sense that the analysis follows the sequence of steps outlined in table 5-5, starting with variance analyses of the three major performance indicators (profitability, growth and productivity) and followed by either partial or comprehensive audit. The method is *selective* in the sense that the decisions with regard to stoppage and the degree of comprehensiveness of the audit are discretionary. As a result, any partial audit is likely to be subjectively selective. The approach is *productivity based* because it requires computation and analysis of total factor productivity changes implicit in the budget. The sequence affords options of either engaging in a partial analysis only or extending it to a full-fledged analysis. Analysts can opt for various degrees of partial analysis. The extension toward a full fledged audit can be done stepwise, after successive analysis of subsystems has been conducted in the sequence signalled by the initial variance analysis of the productivity, profitability and growth indicators.

It is noteworthy that the sequential productivity based auditing approach could be applied, in a modified form, to government and nonprofit organizations, provided that outputs can be identified and quantified, and organizational objectives be operationally defined. Under these circumstances, the computation of the total factor productivity gain would follow a procedure similar to the one used for profit making enterprises. However, the weights assigned to the individual output components in the total output function will have to be subjective in most instances. The profitability and revenue growth indicators should be substituted by indicators measuring the degree of attainment of the major strategic and operational objectives of the organization.

Notes

1. In zero-base budgeting all proposed budget targets are analyzed from ground zero rather than incrementally (i.e., in terms of changes relative to previous budgeted levels). Full-fledged zero-base budgeting is usually very costly. Consequently, a sequential partial zero-base audit can be very advantageous.
2. In Figure 5-5, Y is a vector of outputs. P is a vector of output prices. X is a vector of inputs and W is a vector of input prices. $\hat{W}$ is a vector of standard input prices, $X(Y)$ is a vector of standard inputs which are contingent on actual outputs. $\tilde{Y}$ is the level of total output and $\tilde{X}$ is the level of total inputs. R is total revenue and W_k is the return on capital.

6 EFFICIENCY MEASURES IN MARKETING

Marketing Objectives and Total Marketing Output

The marketing function is indisputably one of the more important of corporate activities. Products and services may be produced efficiently, but if they are not marketed efficiently, higher level organizational objectives may not be attained. An appropriate marketing concept, strategic marketing planning, sound product positioning, and timely product development and innovation are often essential to the maintenance of acceptable profitability, growth and quality performance. Consequently, a significant share of corporate resources is ordinarily allocated to marketing endeavors designed to inform and motivate customers and to facilitate distribution and sales. It is therefore important for management to be able to assess the efficiency and effectiveness of marketing activities.

Unfortunately, efforts to develop marketing efficiency measures are at an embryonic stage. The major difficulties center around appropriate measures of output. Clearly, marketing in conjunction with other activities of the firm contributes to profits and growth. It is of course a classic case of joint production. Disentangling the unique contribution of marketing activities to quantities of products and services sold and the revenues and profits they generated is an extremely arduous, if not impossible, task. In the absence of good measures of marketing output it is hardly surprising that meaningful indexes of marketing efficiency, their managerial importance nonwithstanding, are hard to come by.

While output in production can be appropriately measured by the physical volume of goods and services produced, the same is not true of marketing output. Marketing efforts affect the demand functions for the products and services involved and therefore produce changes in quantities sold as well as prices charged. Thus, the portions of *revenues* directly generated by marketing inputs are better measures of marketing output than mere quantities. For example, successful marketing can be at times oriented toward upgrading the quality perception of the product, thereby facilitating sale of the same quantity at higher price. The additional revenues generated by price increases of this type should be appropriately recognized as an output of this particular marketing activity.

Broadly speaking, the two major objectives of marketing activity are (a) adding new customers, and (b) retaining old existing customers. The corresponding marketing activities aimed at furthering these twin objectives are expansive marketing and retentive marketing. Following the analytical framework proposed by Jagpal and Sudit (1978), retentive marketing encompasses all marketing actions designed to retain existing customers. Expansive marketing pertains to marketing activities aimed at expanding clientele. The distinction between expansive and retentive marketing, while conceptually sound, may be very difficult to apply in practice. Retentive and expansive marketing are often undertaken and carried out jointly, making precise allocation difficult. Also, distinctions between the acquisition of new customers, expansion of sales to old customers, and efforts aimed directly at increasing sales per customer are often very fuzzy. In spite of practical difficulties, such distinctions are of analytical and strategic importance. Analytically, revenues generated by expansive marketing ought to be estimated by different methods from revenues generated by retentive marketing. This is essential for a correct specification of total marketing output. Strategically, misallocation of resources between retentive and expansive designations, overinvesting in one while underinvesting in the other, may be prevalent. The estimation of the relative economic returns to expansive versus retentive marketing are thus instrumental in the determination of the appropriate marketing instruments mix, thereby providing targets for more efficient allocations of marketing efforts.

Measuring Efficiency in Expansive Marketing

Consider a corporate enterprise with n corporate products or services ($i = 1, \ldots, n$) where C_{io}^{E} is the cost of expansive marketing of the ith service to obtain customers at time $t = 0$ and R_{it}^{E} is the certainty-equivalent net revenue inflow generated by the ith service sold to new customers during period t.[1] The economic efficiency of expansive marketing of the ith product or service, EEM_{io}, is defined by the net present value of the endeavor. This is measured as:

$$EEM_{io} = -C_{io} + \sum_{t=o}^{N} \frac{R_{it}^{E}}{(1 + r)^{t}} \qquad (6.1)$$

where N is the expected average number of years of retaining new customers and r is the estimated opportunity cost of capital.

Thus, EEM_{io} in (6.1) can be defined as measure of the efficiency of expansive marketing. Note that in measuring the efficiency of expansive marketing the time lag effects of a marketing effort have to be allowed for. An expansive marketing activity at time $t = o$ can bring in new customers in future periods via cumulative effects of messages, word of mouth etc. Hence, the benefits of investments in expansive marketing can accrue over a number of future periods. The duration of the forward impact of expansive marketing, N, can be estimated by the number of periods that an average customer is likely to be retained. Such estimates can be based on periodic studies of brand loyalty duration. Given the degree of uncertainty of marketing output returns, it is necessary to measure those future revenue inflows (the R_{it}^{E}s) in terms of certainty equivalents. The certainty equivalent method adjusts the expected value of a return to account for the uncertainty associated with its realization. The adjustment factor is usually based on the variance of the distribution of the outcomes as subjectively evaluated by the decision maker.

Upon analysis of the *EEM* indexes, expansive marketing activities with negative or very low positive marketing efficiency measures should be reorganized or discontinued. For example, a negative *EEM* measure in (6.1) may simply indicate that specific expansive marketing strategies (e.g., advertising campaigns to attract new customers) are inefficient and may have to be changed. Expansive marketing activities should be increased for those products and potential customers that produce relatively high *EEMs*.

Assuming realistically that the funds available for expansive marketing are limited, the optimal rule is to allocate resources among services and accounts to achieve equality of increments to net present values of expansive marketing among all products and services:

$$\Delta EEM_{it}^{E} = \Delta EEM_{jt}^{E} \qquad i \neq j \tag{6.2}$$

where ΔEEM_{it} is the increment to the net present value of expansive marketing for product i induced by an investment of one additonal dollar in the expansive marketing of this product. This approach to expansive marketing should enable management to assess more accurately: (1) the profitability of expansive marketing for each service and, to the extent the data permits, for each customer and (2) the efficiency in allocation of resources for new marketing efforts among services and possibly among customers.

Measuring Efficiency in Retentive Marketing

All marketing activities designed to prevent existing customers from leaving should be categorized as retentive. In practice, however, it is not always possible to distinguish sharply between activities that constitute normal servicing of customers in accordance with acceptable quality standards and efforts specifically directed toward maintaining and improving customer loyalty. Only the latter activities and their associated costs constitute the direct costs of retentive marketing. It may be difficult to unambiguously separate those costs. Expansive and retentive marketing could be complementary as well as substitutable activities. For example, expansive and retentive marketing could reinforce each other's effectiveness via reputation and word of mouth. Such potential synergy implies the possible existence of joint costs, thereby further complicating cost allocations between retentive and expansive efforts.

We now proceed to outline a practical way to assess benefits of retentive marketing. A periodic estimation of brand loyalty of customers by product or service in terms of repeat purchasing and nonswitching to competitors is required. Based on conventional marketing research techniques such estimates of brand loyalty can be obtained. We assume that revenues attributable to repeat purchases of existing customers per period represent the return to retentive marketing efforts for that period. This estimate of the output of retentive marketing assumes that recurring year by year retentive marketing is necessary to safeguard all existing business. Accordingly, the benefit of retentive marketing for the loyal customers of the ith product for time t can be estimated by the certainty equivalent of the net revenue flows generated by these loyal existing customers for the period R^R_{it}. If the related retentive marketing outlay is estimated as C^R_{it}, the efficiency measure of retentive marketing for product i, ERM_i, can be defined as follows:

$$ERM_{it} = -C^R_{it} + R^R_{it} \tag{6.3}$$

Note that ERM_{it} is a crude approximation of a cost benefit efficiency measure of retentive marketing. To the extent that a certain proportion of existing customers is likely to remain loyal without an investment in retentive marketing ERM_{it} overstates the efficiency of retentive marketing. On the other hand, to the extent some customers will be retained for more than one period as a result of a one time retentive marketing effort, ERM_{it} understates the cost benefit efficiency of retentive marketing. In the absence of extensive knowledge of diverse patterns of response of segments of existing customers the net effect of these conflicting biases on ERM_{it} will remain unknown.

Efficiency Measures for Marketing Financial Services: A Case Study (Jagpal and Sudit 1978)

The case study of efficiency analysis of marketing of financial service discussed in this section was reported by Jagpal and Sudit. (1978, pp. 424–42) The analyses of the efficiencies of expansive and retentive marketing effort reported below were conducted on an experimental basis for a trust department of an actual commercial bank in 1975 as an aid to its marketing planning for 1976. Tables 6-1 and 6-2 summarize the results for the Corporate Trust Department of bank X. The department was organized by product (service) lines. Evaluations of expansive marketing efficiency (table 6-1) and retentive marketing efficiency (table 6-2) were completed for five major corporate trust product lines. The product (service) lines of the trust department were: (1) pension trust, (2) investment management, (3) custody, (4) corporate trust, and (5) agency.

The estimated cost of expansive marketing for 1976 is shown in column one of table 6-1. Product managers were asked to allocate their total planned marketing outlay, primarily marked for personal selling, between investment in expansive marketing and retentive marketing efforts. The allocation was done on the basis of the time spent by marketing personnel for each of the two activities, based on past experience and judgmental estimates of future practice. The product managers were also asked to estimate the number and size of new accounts expected to be acquired during 1976 and their expected

Table 6-1. Corporate Trust Department of Bank X: Expansive (New) Marketing Cost-Benefit

Trust Product/Service	*Estimated Cost* of New Marketing (1)*	*Marginal Rate of Funds (%) (2)*	*Expected Annual New Revenues* (3)*	*Average Age of Accounts (Years) (4)*	*Present Value* (5)*	*Net Present Value* (6) = (5) − (1)*
Pension trust	90	7	21	8	125	+35
Investment management	160	6	58	3	155	−5
Custody	70	7	8	11	60	−10
Corporate trust	110	8	32	15	274	+164
Agency (stock transfer)	55	6	9	4	29	−26

*In thousands of U.S. dollars.
Source: Jagpal and Sudit (1978).

Table 6-2. Corporate Trust Department of Bank X: Retentive Marketing Cost-Benefit

Trust Product/Service	*Estimated Cost* of Retentive Marketing (1)*	*Marginal Rate of Funds (%) (2)*	*Annual Net Revenues* (3)*	*Cumulative Effect (Years) (4)*	*Present Value* (5)*	*Net Present Value* (6) = (5) − (1)*
Pension trust	60	5.5	72	1	72	+12
Investment management	85	5.5	158	1	158	+73
Custody	40	5.5	(20,10)	2	29	−11
Corporate trust	65	6.0	(97,62,30)	3	177	+112
Agency	85	5.5	90	1	90	+5

*In thousands of U.S. dollars.
Source: Jagpal and Sudit (1978).

aggregate annual net revenue stream (column three, table 6-1). The net revenue flows do not vary over the years since it was assumed that increases in servicing and production costs could be offset by higher fees. It was also assumed that the newly added accounts are likely to stay approximately as long as the average age of existing accounts in each product category (column four, table 6.1). The expected value of the marginal rate of funds during the average life period was used as a discount factor reflecting opportunity costs. The variability in the discount factor among products is attributable to the variability of the expected average age values of new accounts in each product category.[2] The present value of the planned expansive marketing effort for each product is computed in column five of table 6-1. The estimated *net* present value of the 1976 planned expansive marketing per product is derived in column six of the same table. The expected value of the marginal rate of funds reflects expectations at the margin about the future cost of funds and is therefore likely to vary with the life of an account.

The computation of efficiency measures for retentive marketing is summarized in table 6-2. The estimated planned investment levels in retentive marketing are shown in column one. Annual net revenues (column three) are the estimated net revenue inflows for existing accounts in 1976. The product managers expected cumulative carry-over effects in subsequent periods for the custody and corporate trust product lines. For custody trusts, a carry-over effect into the second year of accounts generating 50 percent of the revenues was expected. For corporate trust, a two-thirds carry-over into the second year and one-third carry-over into the third year were expected. The annual net revenues for these product lines were projected accordingly on the prorated basis (column three), with the second and the third numbers in the parentheses representing carry-overs to the second and third periods respectively. The present value and net present values of 1976 planned retentive marketing for each product line are derived in columns five and six.

An analysis of the results in tables 6-1 and 6-2 suggests some degree of excessive investment in expansive marketing for investment management, custody and agency, overinvestment in retentive marketing of custody, and possible overinvestment in retentive marketing of pension trust and agency. These tentative observations led to the examination of the following alternative options of resource allocation in trust marketing: (1) greater emphasis on expansive marketing of corporate trust services, using some personnel hours previously committed to agency and custody, (2) reallocating part of the planned investment-management effort from expansive marketing to retentive marketing and (3) temporary freezing of most marketing activities for the agency and custody product lines pending a complete reevaluation of the marketing positioning of these products. The consideration of the third option was prompted by the negative returns on the overall marketing efforts for these product lines.

Selection of an Efficient Mix of Marketing Instruments

Retentive and expansive marketing are each comprised of a set of marketing instruments (e.g. advertising, promotion, personal selling, distribution etc.). The broader problem of marketing efficiency relates to the allocation of resources among those instruments. Efficient allocation of marketing efforts should ultimately be oriented toward approaching the optimal marketing mix (i.e., the composition of investments in marketing instruments which maximize the net present value of the total marketing investment undertaken by the firm).

In this section we propose a method for selecting an efficient mix of marketing instruments which is based on econometric estimation of instrument-sales response functions. Instrument-sales response functions relate dollar sales or revenues (the dependent variable) to dollar investment levels in marketing instruments (the independent variables). The optimal allocation of the marketing instruments is determined on the basis of the estimated parameters of these functions.

For illustration purposes, let us consider an instrument-sales response function with one marketing instrument—advertising. It will become clear throughout the discussion that our approach is readily extendable to the multi-instrument case. The exposition in this section is an abbreviated version of the methodology developed by Jagpal et al. (1982).

Consider, for the sake of simplicity, the case of firm varying only one instrument, advertising, over time. A general advertising sales response function takes the form $R_t = f(A_t, A_{t+1}, \ldots, A_{t-\lambda})$ where R_t are the revenues at period t, and A_t is the level of advertising at time t. Advertising, like most marketing instruments, exhibits, in general, carry-over (intertemporal) effects. The specification of the general advertising—sales response function suggested above allows for maximum advertising carryover effects of λ periods. Jagpal et al. (1982) suggests the specification of the general and very flexible translog functional form. Consider therefore the following advertising sales response function:

$$\ln R_t = \alpha_0 + \Sigma_i \alpha_i \ln A_{t-i} + \sum_{\substack{i,j \\ i \neq j}} \alpha_{ij} \ln A_{t-i} \ln A_{t-j} + \Sigma_i \alpha_{ii} (\ln A_{t-i})^2, \qquad (i,j = 0, 1, \ldots, \lambda) \tag{6.4}$$

where the α's are parameters. Hence the marginal elasticity of current sales with respect to advertising i periods ago is

$$\varepsilon_i = \frac{\partial(\ln R_t)}{\partial(\ln A_{t-i})} = \alpha_i + \sum_{\substack{j \\ j \neq i}} \alpha_{ij} \ln A_{t-j} + 2\alpha_{ii} \ln A_{t-i} \qquad (i,j = 1, \ldots, \lambda) \tag{6.5}$$

and its marginal sales productivity

$$MP_i = \varepsilon_i \frac{R_t}{a_{t-i}} \tag{6.6}$$

The marginal elasticity, ε_i, measures the percentage change in revenues at time t induced by a small percentage change in the level of advertising outlays i periods ago. The marginal productivity, MP_i, measures the incremental dollar change in revenues from sales at time t induced by a one dollar change in the level of advertising outlays i periods ago. Since revenues from sales are viewed as marketing output, the MP_i expression in (6.6) is interpreted as an indicator of the marginal productivity of a marketing instrument (e.g., advertising). As can be seen from equations (6.5) and (6.6) the translog advertising sales response function allows, in general, for the intertemporal dependence of advertising effects by making the marginal elasticities and marginal productivities depend on the time path of advertising spending.

Jagpal et al., used the translog specification in (6.5) to measure the advertising sales response function for the Lydia Pinkham company. They chose monthly sales advertising data for the January 1954 to June 1960 period, since the marketing mix for the company (except for advertising) was relatively stable over this period. This type of stability reduced the likelihood of specification errors due to the possibility of overlooking the effects of omitted independent variables (e.g., other marketing instruments) on revenues. On the basis of elaborate regression tests a two period advertising lag model was selected as representing the best statistical fit.[3] In other words, it was estimated on the basis of statistical testing that any significant carry-over effects of advertising on sales probably lasted for no longer than two periods into the future.

The marginal productivities of advertising for the Lydia Pinkham company were computed by Jagpal et al., on the basis of their estimates of the parameters of the translog function. These marginal productivities for each month are presented in table 6-3. $MP_0(t)$, $MP_1(t)$ and $MP_2(t)$ for any particular month represent respectively the marginal productivities of advertising outlays in the current period, one period ago and two periods ago. Consider, for example, the month of June 1954. One additional dollar of advertising expenditure in June 1954 contributed \$0.5325 to revenues in that month. The May 1954 marginal dollar of advertising induced \$0.5711 in additional revenues in June 1954, while an April 1954 incremental dollar of advertising prompted on \$0.0149 of revenues in June 1954. This information is obtained by reading the numbers for $MP_0(t)$, $MP_1(t)$ and $MP_2(t)$ in the June 1954 row of table 6-3.

The fifth column in table 6-3 measures the total marginal revenue yield, $R_c(t)$, of an incremental dollar of advertising at time t. In other words, $R_c(t)$ measures the total dollar impact on current and future revenues of a marginal dollar of current advertising. Therefore, in the context of the two period advertising model, $R_c(t)$ can be stated as follows:

$$R_c^t = \frac{\partial R_t}{\partial A_t} + \frac{\partial R_{t+1}}{\partial A_t} + \frac{\partial R_{t+2}}{\partial A_t} = MP_0(t) + MP_1(t+1) + MP_2(t+2) \tag{6.7}$$

For example, the total marginal yield for advertising for the month of June 1954 is R_c (June) = MP_0 (June) + MP_1 (July) + MP_2 (August) = 0.5325 + 1.0341 + 0.1444 = 1.7110.

This means the cumulative impact of an additional investment of one dollar in advertising translated into \$1.7110 increment to revenues over the June-August period. The monthly time value of money was assumed to be too small to warrant the discounting of the July and the August marginal productivities to their June present values.

The results in table 6-3 show that the total yield on a marginal dollar of advertising, $R_c(t)$ was less than one dollar for most periods. These results, suggesting a high incidence of over-advertising on the part of the company, are not surprising given that Lydia Pinkham had an average sales advertising ratio of 50% over the entire period. The company's total expense exclusive of advertising averaged 25% of sales. It appears however that the company did under-advertise in some months in terms of the incremental contribution to profits.

The Jagpal et al. findings suggest that econometric analysis based on historical data can provide meaningful estimated measures of advertising

Table 6-3. Marginal Sales Productivities ($MP(t)$) and Total Marginal Yield ($R_c(t)$) of Advertising for the Two Period Model

		Advertising (in 000's)	$MP_0(t)$	$MP_1(t)$	$MP_2(t)$	$R_c(t)$
1954	March	982	0.0551	0.0781	0.0215	0.1684
	April	919	0.0509	0.0939	0.0174	0.1405
	May	87	0.3860	0.0747	0.0194	1.0188
	June	39	0.5325	0.5711	0.0149	1.7110
	July	72	0.2445	1.0341	0.0617	1.2794
	August	467	0.0656	0.8573	0.1444	0.2958
	September	1170	0.0396	0.1864	0.1776	0.1363
	October	917	0.0525	0.0781	0.0438	0.1616
	November	701	0.1616	0.0932	0.0185	0.1604
	December	128	0.2149	0.0804	0.0164	0.7902
1955	January	1014	0.0280	0.4633	0.0184	0.1321
	February	1274	0.0342	0.0800	0.1120	0.1313
	March	1388	0.0373	−.0786	0.0241	0.1213
	April	1071	0.0447	0.0671	0.0185	0.1453
	May	537	0.0837	0.0833	0.0169	0.2342
	June	123	0.2661	0.1268	0.0173	0.7474
	July	60	0.3813	0.4192	0.0237	1.4246
	August	351	0.0706	0.8770	0.0621	0.3345
	September	1061	0.0365	0.2086	0.1663	0.1379
	October	791	0.0595	0.0849	0.0553	0.1560
	November	138	0.2288	0.0815	0.0165	0.6185
	December	77	0.2630	0.3293	0.0149	1.1677
1956	January	1000	0.0280	0.7445	0.0604	0.1300
	February	1182	0.0354	0.0772	0.1602	0.1435
	March	1225	0.0427	0.0859	0.0248	0.1446
	April	936	0.0571	0.0851	0.0222	0.1615
	May	625	0.0646	0.0855	0.0168	0.1856
	June	60	0.5045	0.1014	0.0189	1.4205
	July	61	0.3406	0.8261	0.0196	1.2170
	August	169	0.1300	0.7635	0.0899	0.5560
	September	946	0.0300	0.3255	0.1129	0.1498
	October	1306	0.0375	0.0971	0.1005	0.1151
	November	426	0.1004	0.0642	0.0227	0.2736
	December	88	0.3302	0.1453	0.0134	0.1680
1957	January	1104	0.0267	0.7000	0.0279	0.1138
	February	1093	0.0362	0.0661	0.1378	0.1428
	March	1080	0.0444	0.0856	0.0210	0.1484
	April	1080	0.0468	0.0857	0.0210	0.1413

Table 6-3. *(continued)*

		Advertising (in 000's)	$MP_0(t)$	$MP_1(t)$	$MP_2(t)$	$R_c(t)$
	May	745	0.0537	0.0777	0.0183	0.1534
	June	78	0.3768	0.0816	0.0168	1.1309
	July	66	0.3415	0.6768	0.0181	1.1126
	August	94	0.2162	0.6683	0.0773	0.9516
	September	774	0.0369	0.6074	0.1028	0.1495
	October	971	0.0402	0.0942	0.1280	0.1206
	November	536	0.0555	0.0602	0.0184	0.2083
	December	150	0.2378	0.1375	0.0202	0.5497
1958	January	580	0.0314	0.2533	0.0153	0.1469
	February	1121	0.0234	0.0858	0.0586	0.1068
	March	974	0.0401	0.0671	0.0297	0.1352
	April	1002	0.0374	0.0755	0.0163	0.1220
	May	138	0.2538	0.0706	0.0196	0.6803
	June	72	0.3172	0.3748	0.0140	0.9604
	July	59	0.3105	0.5696	0.0517	1.1996
	August	270	0.0772	0.7434	0.0736	0.3832
	September	986	0.0347	0.2415	0.1457	0.1364
	October	673	0.0653	0.0852	0.0645	0.1786
	November	304	0.1031	0.0941	0.0165	0.3113
	December	209	0.1216	0.1741	0.0192	0.4361
1959	January	838	0.0318	0.2565	0.0341	0.1296
	February	994	0.0332	0.0747	0.0580	0.1339
	March	1020	0.0407	0.0812	0.0231	0.1362
	April	865	0.0464	0.0771	0.0195	0.1523
	May	819	0.0471	0.0878	0.0184	0.1325
	June	83	0.3381	0.0703	0.0181	0.9675
	July	56	0.3555	0.5648	0.0151	1.2260
	August	224	0.0874	0.7462	0.0646	0.3921
	September	881	0.0324	0.2442	0.1243	0.1220
	October	436	0.0792	0.0752	0.0605	0.2163
	November	160	0.1467	0.1118	0.0144	0.4712
	December	68	0.3108	0.2897	0.0253	0.8836
1960	January	749	0.0235	0.05380	0.0348	0.1241
	February	857	0.0371	0.0788	0.1337	0.1368
	March	898	0.0393	0.0804	0.0218	0.1334
	April	705	0.0489	0.0754	0.0193	0.1647
	May	489	0.0694	0.0961	0.0187	
	June	59	0.4183	0.1061	0.0197	

Source: Jagpal et al. (1982).

efficiency for planning and control purpose. Alternatively, advertising efficiency can be estimated by controlled experimentation, provided that such experimentation is not too costly, risky, or time consuming in relation to its expected informational benefits. Regardless of data collection methods and estimations techniques, however, marginal productivity analysis can be a useful tool in evaluating the efficiency of intertemporal allocation of marketing efforts.

Generally speaking, the econometric approach to marketing efficiency analysis is readily extendable to the multi-instrument case. For instance, the translog specification in equation (6.4) can, in principle, accommodate several independent variables. Consequently, all relevant marketing instruments can be specified as explanatory variables. These multi-instrument sales response functions lend themselves to marginal productivity analysis capable of evaluating the efficiency of intertemporal, as well as interinstrument allocation of marketing resources. However, specifications of numerous marketing instruments and generalized functional forms tend to increase the number of independent variables, which, in turn, require larger data samples and more complex statistical estimation techniques. Thus, the scope and applicability of econometric marketing efficiency analysis is likely to be constrained to some degree by considerations of data availability and statistical validity. Multi-instrument sales response functions can be also estimated for joint multi-input multi-output formulations allowing for a joint use of marketing instruments to promote simultaneously sales of several products. Jagpal and Sudit (1980) used multivariate statistical techniques to estimate the marginal sales productivities of joint marketing efforts. Such joint models make it possible to select, evaluate and control efficient instrument mixes for jointly marketing a number of products and services. Marketing instruments can be defined in terms of the types of marketing activities (e.g., advertising, personal selling etc.) and/or in terms of the goals of those activities (e.g., expansive marketing vs. retentive marketing).

Notes

1. A *net revenue inflow* is defined, for the purpose of our discussion in this chapter, as the cash flow of revenues generated during a certain period by a particular marketing effort minus the marketing related cash outflows generated by required marketing expenses for the same period.

2. Since the marginal rate of funds was expected to rise gradually in the future, a higher discount factor was applied to revenues of new accounts in product lines for which a higher average life per account was expected.

3. For a detailed exposition of statistical analysis see Jagpal et al. (1982).

7 PRODUCTIVITY BASED MANAGEMENT OF INTERNATIONAL OPERATIONS

International Differences in Productivity Growth

Productivity growth rates and patterns differ significantly between countries over the very long term as well as over short periods of time. In general, the reasons for these pronounced differences in national productivities are obvious. Countries vary enormously in their human resources, natural resources, capital resources, culture, institutions and organization of production. Attempts at a methodical accounting of the sources of different rates of international growth rates have been undertaken by Denison (1967), who provides important insight into the international role of productivity in economic growth.

To illustrate the magnitude of international differences in productivity advances we first examine differences in annual rates of growth in real national product per year worked for thirteen countries over more than half a century. Table 7-1 shows that even for very long periods productivity advances differ significantly. For example, U.S. annual rates of growth in output per year worked for the period 1871–1959 was 60% higher than that of the U.K. for the period 1857–1959, while the Japanese rate of growth for the period 1880–1959 was more than double that of the U.K. The variability

Table 7-1. Recent and Long-Term Growth Rates in Real National Product per Year Worked and Output per Hour in Manufacturing. Thirteen Countries (average annual percentage rates of change)

	(A) *Real National Product per Year Worked*			*(B)* *Output per Hour in Manufacturing*
Country	*Starting Year*	*To 1959*	*1950–59*	*1960–75*
Japan	1880	2.9	6.1	9.7
Italy	1863	1.2	4.7	6.2
Germany	1853	1.5	4.5	5.7
France	1855	1.5	3.6	5.6
Netherlands	1900	1.1	3.4	7.1
Norway	1865	1.6	3.1	n.a
Sweden	1863	2.1	2.8	6.6
United States	1871	2.0	2.2	2.7
Canada	1872	1.7	2.0	4.0
Denmark	1872	1.6	1.8	7.2
United Kingdom	1857	1.2	1.7	3.8
Belgium	—	n.a	n.a	7.0
Switzerland	—	n.a	n.a	5.1

n.a. = not available.
Source: Kendrick (1977, p. 56).

in productivity advances for shorter periods is much greater (see table 7-1 columns three and four).

The differential impact of diverse growth patterns in output per hour of twelve countries during 1970–75 on unit labor costs is underscored in table 7-2. For example, West Germany's annual growth rate in output per hour during 1970–75 was triple that of the U.S., while its growth in unit labor costs was more than double the U.S. rate of growth in unit labor costs in U.S. dollar terms.

The variability in partial productivity growth rates among industrial countries, however, does not tell the full productivity story. Advances in output per hour can vary due to different rates of growth in capital. Thus the international comparisons among rates of total factor productivities, as summarized in tables 7-3 and 7-4, are more appropriate. Upon examining these tables it becomes clear that the variability in TFP advances among countries is as large for TFP growth patterns as it is for growth rates in partial productivity indexes. This pattern of variability in productivity performance

Table 7-2. Comparative Rates of Change in Productivity, Average Earnings, and Unit Labor Costs. Twelve Countries 1970-75 (average annual percentage rates of change)

			Unit Labor Costs	
Country	*Output per hour*	*Average Hourly Compensation*	*National Currency*	*U.S. Dollars*
United States	1.8	8.0	6.1	6.1
Canada	2.7	10.0	7.1	7.8
Japan	5.4	20.7	14.5	19.8
Belgium	7.6	26.9	8.7	16.1
Denmark	6.8	15.5	8.1	14.7
France	3.4	15.1	11.4	17.3
West Germany	5.4	13.3	7.5	17.3
Italy	6.0	22.1	15.2	14.0
Netherlands	5.8	26.0	9.7	18.6
Sweden	5.0	14.1	8.7	13.9
Switzerland	3.5	11.9	8.2	20.3
United Kingdom	3.1	16.4	12.9	11.2

Source: Kendrick (1977, p. 59).

is maintained regardless of whether conventional TFP methods are used (table 7-3) or dynamic residuals are computed (table 7-4).

It is also noteworthy that TFP changes for all countries are very important in explaining changes in their respective outputs. This is best illustrated by the fact that for most countries the rates of growth in TFP are higher than the rates of growth in total inputs (real factor inputs), as illustrated in table 7-3. The means that productivity changes have often a greater impact on total output than the combined effects of changes in underlying inputs.

The importance of TFP growth in accounting for changes in output has been demonstrated in numerous studies of national economies, sectors, industries and companies. The variability in international TFP growth rates among industries is generally greater than the observed variability among macro-level national productivity advances. The pronounced industry differences across countries in productivity performances play a very important role in international trade decisions. In effect, differences in relative productivities are major sources of comparative advantages among countries. If an industry in country *A* is more productive in producing certain products than the same industry in country *B*, then country *A* is likely to

Table 7-3. Average Annual Growth Rates of Real Product, Real Factor Inputs, and Total Factor Productivity

	Canada	*France*	*West Germany*	*Italy*	*Japan*	*Korea*	*Nether-lands*	*United Kingdom*	*United States*
	1947–73	1950–73	1950–73	1952–73	1952–73		1951–73	1955–73	1947–73
Real property	.051	.055	.064	.052	.098	—	.053	.037	.038
Real factor input	.034	.025	.029	.024	.057	—	.029	.017	.027
Total factor productivity	.017	.030	.036	.029	.041	—	.025	.019	.013
Real capital input	.058	.056	.070	.045	.088	—	.055	.045	.043
Real labor input	.015	.004	.003	.010	.035		.008	.000	.016
	1947–60	1950–60	1950–60	1952–60	1952–60		1951–60	1955–60	1947–60
Real product	.051	.048	.082	.060	.081	—	.048	.033	.036
Real factor input	.035	.020	.036	.026	.047	—	.027	.018	.025
Total factor productivity		.029	.047	.033	.033	—	.023	.015	.014
Real capital input	.068	.047	.069	.033	.044	—	.040	.044	.046
Real labor input	.011	.003	.016	.022	.048	—	.014	.002	.012
	1960–73								
Real product	.051	.059	.050	.047	.109	.097	.056	.038	.041
Real factor input	.033	.029	.024	.022	.064	.058	.030	.018	.029
Total factor productivity	.018	.030	.028	.025	.045	.040	.025	.021	.012
Real capital input	.049	.063	.070	.054	.115	.072	.066	.046	.040
Real labor input	.020	.004	.007	.002	.027	.050	.003	.000	.022

Source: Hulten and Nishimizu (1980).

Table 7-4. Average Annual Growth Rates of Intertemporal Output, Input, and the Dynamic Residual

	Canada	*France*	*West Germany*	*Italy*	*Japan*	*Korea*	*Netherlands*	*United Kingdom*	*United States*
	1947–73	1950–73	1950–73	1952–73	1952–73		1951–73	1955–73	1947–73
Real wealth	.057	.060	.064	.062	.113	—	.065	.034	.046
Value added by labor	.014	.004	.004	.011	.033	—	.008	.001	.015
Dynamic residual	.043	.056	.061	.051	.080	—	.057	.033	.031
	1947–60	1950–60	1950–60	1952–60	1952–60		1951–60	1955–60	1947–60
Real wealth	.060	.061	.092	.081	.118	—	.071	.031	.044
Value added by labor	.011	.003	.016	.022	.048	—	.015	.002	.011
Dynamic residual	.049	.058	.076	.059	.070	—	.056	.029	.034
	1960–1973								
Real wealth	.053	.060	.038	.047	.110	.117	.060	.036	.050
Value added by labor	.019	.005	−.008	.002	.025	.049	.003	.001	.022
Dynamic residual	.034	.055	.046	.045	.085	.068	.058	.035	.028

Source: Hulten and Nishimizu (1980).

exhibit a comparative advantage over B in producing these products. This, in the short run, is likely to affect import and export decisions concerning these products. In the long run, direct investment policies and transfer of technologies in these areas may be affected.

In this chapter we shall explore how information concerning differences in relative productivities of companies and industries across countries can be used to improve export and import decisions, direct investment planning, and technology transfer policies. The discussion below follows, with minor modifications and extensions, Sudit's (1984) analysis.

The Role of Relative Productivities in Export Decisions

Consider firm A in country A selling its product in country B. Firm's A profit from this export, Π^{AB}, can be stated as:

$$\Pi^{AB} = \rho P^{AB}\, Y^{AB} - C(Y^{AB}) \tag{7.1}$$

where P^{AB} is the price charged by firm A in country B. Y^{AB} is the quantity that firm A exports to country B. $C(Y^{AB})$ is the total cost of producing A's export to B. ρ is the exchange rate of B in terms of A's currency. Since P^{AB} is quoted in terms of B's currency, ρP^{AB} is the price in A's currency. All production takes place in country A, therefore the total costs $C(Y^{AB})$ is stated in A's currency. Consequently, Π^{AB} is stated in terms of the currency of the exporting country A.

Firm A will maximize profits if it exports at the quantity level Y^{AB} for which its marginal cost equals its marginal revenue. Given that $C(Y^{AB}) = \Sigma_i W_i^A X_i^A$, where X_i^A is the quantity of the i-th input used in A's export production and W_i^A is the respective input price, the first order conditions for profit maximization of (7.1) can be stated as:

$$\rho P^{AB}\left(1 + \frac{1}{\varepsilon_{AB}}\right) = \frac{\Sigma_i W_i^A X_i^A}{Y^{AB}}\,(1 + \phi_A) \tag{7.2}$$

where

$$\varepsilon_{AB} = \frac{d(Y^{AB})}{d(P^{AB})}\,\frac{P^{AB}}{Y^{AB}}$$

is the price elasticity of export demand,

$$\phi_A = \frac{d\left(\dfrac{\Sigma_i W_i^A X_i^A}{Y^{AB}}\right)}{dY^{AB}} \cdot \frac{Y^{AB}}{\Sigma_i W_i^A X_i^A / Y^{AB}}$$

is the elasticity of the average cost of export production with respect to its quantity, or the elasticity of export supply.[1]

Rearranging (7.2) we obtain:

$$\rho P^{AB} = \frac{(1 + \phi_A)}{\left(1 + \dfrac{1}{\varepsilon_{AB}}\right)} \; \Sigma_i W_i^A \frac{X_i^A}{Y^{AB}} \tag{7.3}$$

where $(1 + \phi_A)/\{1 + (1/\varepsilon_{AB})\}$ is the mark-up factor obtained by A in selling at market B at a profit maximizing level of export. Under these circumstances, export by A and B will be profitable if this mark-up factor is higher or equal to unity. This translates to the following condition:

$$\rho P^{AB} \geq \Sigma_i W_i^A \frac{X_i^A}{Y^{AB}} \tag{7.4}$$

Equation (7.4) states that in order for A to export to B it should realize at least normal economic profits from this operation.[2] Violation of (7.4) would imply "dumping" by firm A in country B since the P^{AB} in (7.4) is the profit maximizing or loss minimizing price required in (7.3), representing the best level of profitability that the exporting firm can attain under the circumstances. A loss minimizing P^{AB} obtained in (7.3) implies that the exporting firm is selling below cost. Thus, the optimal export decision should satisfy conditions (7.3) and (7.4).

The role of productivity in the export decision is underscored by the input requirement ratios, X_i^{AB}/Y^{AB}, $(i = 1, \ldots, n)$. These are the inverses of the partial productivity indexes for the respective inputs. For example, if the i-th input is labor and X_i^A is measured by manhours, then X_i^A/Y^{AB} signifies the number of manhours required by A to produce one unit of output for export to B. The inverse of this ratio, Y^{AB}/X_i^A, is output per manhour or the labor productivity of A. W_i^A will be the compensation per manhour paid by A. The same interpretation will hold for any other input (e.g., capital or raw materials.) Additionally, the term $\Sigma_i W_i^A(X_i^A/Y^{AB})$ can be interpreted as the total factor productivity of A in exporting to B. This TFP measure differs from the Laspeyres TFP index only in that inputs are weighted by current prices rather than constant prices. This type of index measures in effect the changes in total costs per unit of output.

So far, we have established through conditions (7.3) and (7.4) that the profitability of export decisions depend on: (a) the technologically determined partial productivities of its inputs (the X_i^A/Y^{AB} ratios); (b) its input prices (the W_i's); (c) the elasticity of demand for its product in the export market, ε_{AB}, generally reflecting the perceived uniqueness of its product in country B; (d) the elasticity of supply factor, ϕ_A, reflecting A's ability to economize on input prices or achieve increasing returns to scale as it increases the volume of its domestic production: and (e) the rate of exchange, ρ, between country *A* and country *B*. Of these factors, in a regime of flexible exchange rates, even short term variations in ρ may be the most difficult to predict. These difficulties in predicting exchange rate fluctuations are well documented in Levich (1981, 1982), where he shows that only few forecasting services achieved statistically significant results of exceeding 60% accuracy over all currencies. On the other hand, within short to medium time intervals the input requirement or partial productivity ratios could be more stable, lending themselves to technological forecasts, relatively more reliable than the market forecasts of input prices. Very little productivity forecasting is done at present by outside forecasting services. Therefore track records of productivity forecasts are generally unavailable for comparative purposes. However, productivity time series are observed to be generally less volatile than price, unit cost or exchange rate time series. Productivity changes reflect primarily implementation of technical change which generally require significant lead times, thus facilitating better forecasts. Finally, productivity gains are often realized through a process of learning new methods and technologies. Learning curves often display patterns that make forecasting of their effects on productivity somewhat more reliable. It therefore should not be too difficult for firms to generate internal forecasts of relative productivity trends in export industries, in view of the potential importance of relative productivities in international trade. The benefits of such forecasts are likely to be well worth the costs.

Considering the effects of competition in export markets, suppose that similar products to the one exported by *A* to *B* are also manufactured in country *B*. Conditions (7.3) and (7.4) could be restated so as to apply to a profit maximizing firm *B* selling a similar product in market *B*:

$$P^{BB} = \frac{1 + \phi_B}{1 + \dfrac{1}{\varepsilon_{BB}}} \, \Sigma_i W_i^B \, \frac{X_i^B}{Y^{BB}} \qquad (7.5)$$

so that:

$$P^{BB} \geq \Sigma_i W_i^B \frac{X_i^B}{Y^{BB}} \qquad (7.6)$$

Where P^{BB} is the price charged by firm *B* in Market *B* and Y^{BB} is the quantity produced by firm *B* for sale in market *B*, ε_{BB} is the price elasticity of demand in market *B* for the product of firm *B*. The definitions for X_i^B, W_i^B and

ϕ_B are analogous to the definitions for X_i^A, W_i^A *and* ϕ_A above. Clearly, $\rho = 1$ when firm B sells in the country it operates in.

If there are many firms in country B producing products similar to A we can regard the variables in (7.5) and (7.6) as pertaining to the average or representative firm in B. When these products are *homogeneous* ($\varepsilon_{BB} = \infty$ and $\varepsilon_{AB} = \infty$), a necessary condition for the *profitability* of A's exports is:

$$P^{AB} \leq P^{BB} \tag{7.7}$$

Invoking (7.3) and (7.5), subject to $\varepsilon_{AB} = \infty$ and $\varepsilon_{BB} = \infty$, condition (7.7) can be restated as:

$$\frac{1}{\rho}(1 + \phi_A)\Sigma_i W_i^A \frac{X_i^A}{Y^{AB}} \leq (1 + \phi_B)\Sigma_i W_i^B \frac{X_i^B}{Y^{BB}} \tag{7.8}$$

Condition (7.8) implies that if products are homogeneous, it is the relationship between the average cost of production (at the optimal levels of of output) between countries A and B which assume major importance. In perfectly competitive markets, assuming no transportation or transaction costs, (7.8) alone is necessary for a profitable export of A. Equation (7.8) together with (7.5) and (7.6) are necessary and sufficient for a profitable export of A.[3] Furthermore, as long as markets are perfectly competitive it is also sufficient for firm A to establish that conditions (7.8) and (7.6) hold. Condition (7.6) guarantees that the representative firm B is profitable in B. Thus, (7.5) is profit maximizing. The advantage of ascertaining (7.6) and (7.8) for decision making purposes is that in perfectly competitive markets firm A can establish the profitability of exporting its product to B on the basis of relative costs and the profitability of competitive B firms without the need to resort to estimation of the demand in market B for its own product.

If products are sufficiently diversified (nonhomogeneous) then (7.5), (7.6), and (7.8) are neither sufficient nor necessary conditions for the profitability of A's export. The magnitude of the price elasticity for A's product in market B must be taken into account. For example, conditions (7.3) and (7.5) may hold while (7.4) is violated if the perceived uniqueness of product A translates to a sufficiently low price elasticity of demand ε_{AB}. This allows for the role of product attributes and marketing in exporting a diversified product. It should however be remembered that the demand for A's product in market B and its price elasticity will be affected by the prices of the substitute B product P^{BB}.[4] Hence, the relative costs of production in countries A and B indirectly affect the demand for A in B.

The importance of the balance between average costs in countries A and B in export decision is evident from our previous discussion. Condition (7.8) underscores the role of the partial productivities or input requirements. The exporting firm has no control over input prices in country *B*, and usually little, if any, control over its own input prices. As for the exchange rate ρ, for short term export decisions the risk associated with flexible exchange rates can be either eliminated or reduced by hedging in the future markets for currencies. In long term export decisions, exchange rate levels are beyond control and very difficult to predict. Thus, from the view point of Firm *A*, the most estimatable and often the more controllable variables are likely to be its partial productivities (Y^{AB}/X_i^A, $i = 1, \ldots, n$) and its economies of scale ϕ_A. Furthermore, the partial productivities and economies of scale for the average *B* firm lend themselves to more reliable and accurate predictions than input prices or exchange rates. Relative technological trends are simply more stable and the underlying basic technological factors are better known. It is therefore important for the exporting firm to supplement its demand cost and exchange rate analyses by a continuous and forward looking examination of its productivity levels and trends relative to foreign competition. A *more favorable outlook for profitable exports is usually generated when firm* A *has a significant overall productivity advantage over the average or representative* B *firm.* Overall relative productivity is defined as a condition under which most or all input requirements of firm *A* are significantly lower than for the average *B* firm. Otherwise, *A*'s export profitability will solely depend on such relatively volatile factors as relative wages, relative interest rates, exchange rates, demand elasticities and cross elasticities. Consequently, ascertaining a high probability of preserving positive future productivity, differentials based on current overall productivity advantages are particularly important for long term export decision (i.e., when long term productivity differentials based on current overall productivity advantages and growing export positioning.) Moreover, the mere absence of a relative productivity advantage on the part of firm *A*, let alone the uncovering of a productivity disadvantage, may signal potential future trouble. Such conditions could, in time, provide incentives for *B* firms to make inroads or increase their market shares in country *A*, at the expense of firm *A*. Profitability, or lack of it, in export decisions could be symmetric, affecting *B* firm's decision in a manner similar to *A*'s. It is thus important to realize that relative productivity advantages provide firms with safety margins in the event of changes in other market variables pertinent to their competitive positions (e.g., changes in relative factor prices). In a dynamic sense, maintenance of relative productivity advantages could also give firms some lead time to adjust to adverse relative changes in monetary variables without incurring actual losses or jeopardizing their market positions.

In the context of relative productivity analysis it is noteworthy that all factors of production other than primary inputs are produced by other factors. Following Sraffa's (1960) analysis of the production of commodities by other commodities, it should be explicitly recognized that relative price movements in different industries, sectors or countries are determined by a long sequence of production processes. Average prices of inputs in foreign and domestic industries are determined largely by the productivities underlying their respective production processes. For example the relationship between input prices in country *B* and the underlying productivity of their production can be stated as follows:

$$W_i^B = \sum_{ji} V_{ji}^B \frac{Z_{ji}^B}{X_i^B} \tag{7.9}$$

where Z_{ji}^B and V_{ji}^B are respectively the quantity and price of the *j*-th input used to produce the *i*-th input in country *B* ($j = 1, \ldots, n$). In turn, similar relationships to those in (7.9) can be developed for the V_{ji}'s, provided the input industries are competitive and exhibit constant returns to scale.

This line of reasoning posits that the foreign price movements of the product, which determine export allocations, are dependent on the cumulative effects of relative input requirements or productivity patterns in a long sequence of industries starting from the input industries and tracing backward to the production of the inputs, the inputs of the inputs, etc. Theoretically, the analysis can trace the sequence of production processes back to primary inputs (e.g., natural resources and labor inputs combined to produce the initial capital goods). These underlying relative primary input requirements and their relative prices in the foreign and domestic economies can be interpreted as indicators of the basic comparative advantages, as they relate to the products under consideration for export.[5]

Input-output tables can be of considerable help in tracing input requirements of, say, industry *B* throughout a succession of input industries in the path of production of the final *B* product.[6] Good illustrations of the role of input-output tables in analyzing industrial efficiency are provided by Nyitrai (1976) and Ivanyi (1976). In terms of our model, the input requirement coefficients are directly available from input-output tables. This analysis is limited however by the fact that the input-output tables are compiled only at relatively long intervals. Inbetween smaller tables are available for fewer sectors at high levels of aggregation. Thus, the decision maker is faced with the necessity to estimate and forecast the trends in those coefficients. In this context, it may be feasible to forecast trends in total factor productivities for the relevant input industries, using dynamic input-output models based on successive input-output tables, industry productivity studies, econometric sectoral models, engineering-based technological estimates and company cost accounting quantitative standards.

Oligopolistic Markets and Politization

Our analytical framework for productivity based export decisions would be incomplete if we did not allow for the potential and actual effects of protectionist governmental intervention often designed to mitigate the socio-economic consequences of strong drives by exporting firms to exploit strong relative productivity advantages.

In oligopolistic markets the strategic position of the exporting firm may be complicated by the prospect of politization. Politization occurs when local competitors and unions form coalitions with their governments to counteract import inroads through protectionist measures. As a result, the exporter is likely to modify conventional oligopolistic strategies to allow for prospects for politization. Failure to do so may result in faulty export policies and severe economic penalties.

When an exporter gains a relatively large share of the foreign market the oligopolistic game with his domestic competition is more often than not politicized. The exporter's pricing policies in foreign markets are perceived in terms of their impact on domestic employment in the relevant industries. For example, productivity and/or elasticity considerations may induce the exporting firm to reduce its prices relative to domestic competition. So long as its market share in the foreign market is relatively small the strategic implications of such prices in terms of counter reactions by competitors are likely to be minimal. As its market share increases, the classic oligopolistic market game is often politicized. A coalition of domestic competitors and the domestic labor unions involved are likely to be motivated to appeal for government protective measures in the forms of quotas and tariffs. Loss of employment in the particular industry and its ripple effects on employment levels in the underlying input industries will be cited as a justification for government protection. Thus, in oligopolistic markets the export decision is often broadened, to encompass strategic as well as national industrial policy elements.

The oligopolistic import-export game can be further complicated by the interests of the government of the exporting firm in viewing exports as employment boosters, sources of foreign currencies, and means in maintaining favorable trade accounts. These interests may lead to governmental export incentives, and, in turn, import tariffs and quotas spurred by charges and apprehensions about "dumping" by trade partners. Oligopolistic import-export competitions may thus evolve into all too familiar international trade disputes among governments. A case in point is documented by Tsurumi and Tsurumi (1980). They note that the controversy over imports of Japanese color TV sets to the U.S. may have been stimulated by U.S. color TV manufacturers to buy time to correct managerial, marketing and production mistakes. In October 1977, after Japanese firms were pressured to abide by self-imposed quotas, presumably to save jobs for U.S. workers, Zenith moved its color TV production to subsidiaries in Mexico and Taiwan to compensate for lower wages and higher productivity of its Japanese competitors.

From the point of view of the exporting firm the prospect of governmental trade disputes brings about an additional strong element of uncertainty. In fact, the prospect for political conflicts of this nature is heightened the larger the productivity edge the decision making firm possesses vis à vis its foreign competition. The reason for this correlation is inherent in the difficulties that may be experienced by the foreign competitors, at least in the short run, in their efforts to overcome relative productivity disadvantages. Such difficulties could limit their options for a successful oligopolistic market response and increase pressure for government protection. For the exporting firm the consequences of protective intervention by the host government are highly unpredictable and rarely favorable. Managements with a degree of foresight should contemplate risk reduction strategies in advance. A preventive course of action would be to establish foreign operations in foreign markets either by building plants or by acquiring interest in competitive foreign firms.

The scene in the U.S. automobile market in the late seventies and the early eighties may be a case in point. The longer term interests of Japanese car importers to the U.S. might have been better served had most of them established some form of U.S. operations to forestall or modify the consequences of protectionist moves. It is reasonable to assume that the establishment of U.S. operations by Volkswagen and the purchase of a commanding interest in American Motors by Renault and the GM-Toyota co-production project were motivated in part by these considerations. By contrast, in other products the Japanese have moved first toward U.S. production. For example, Sony and Panasonic, the two Japanese electronics corporations, have built television manufacturing plants in the U.S. Recently, NEC, a subsidiary of the Nippon Electric Company of Tokyo, is undertaking a major investment in a semiconductor manufacturing plant in California aiming at a ten percent share of the semiconductor market by 1986. The postwar movement of American companies to establish local operations in oligopolistic markets abroad is well documented. These strategies can be motivated by (a) higher expected returns due to a combination of comparative technological advantage and lower costs of foreign labor and/or materials; (b) diversification of the production portfolio based on diverse underlying national productivity patterns; (c) reducing the risks of protectionist restrictions spurred by perceived threats to local employment levels. In practice, any one of these factors or the combination of all could constitute the decisive elements in the decision to operate abroad. From a strategic viewpoint it is important to realize that factor (c) alone can often tip the balance in a decision to establish production facilities in foreign markets, provided of course that the export decision to that particular country is reasonably favorable on grounds (a) and/or (b).

In conclusion, the oligopolistic firm can rarely afford to limit its export planning to simple cost benefit decisions based on current demand-cost decisions if it aims at a significant share of the market in any particular foreign country. The productivity based export decision procedures outlined in the preceding sections may have to be supplemented and modified by strategic-political considerations. These may dictate restrained market share targets, establishment of foreign operations and cooperative ventures abroad which may be inconsistent with short term considerations but serve longer term interests.

Productivity Based Diversification of International Investments

So far, the fact that when export decisions are made, future foreign and domestic prices for the product under consideration are likely to be uncertain, has been sidestepped in our analysis. This led to all-or-nothing export-domestic allocation decisions. Allowing for price uncertainties and assuming that the decision maker considers numerous domestic and foreign markets, we can conceive of the export decision as a portfolio problem. With less than perfect correlation among prices in foreign and domestic markets the decision making firm can reduce the overall variation in prices it is confronted with by expanding to foreign markets. A correlation of less than unity is of course very likely even under competitive conditions, flexible exchange rates, and the absence of any trade barriers. Thus, for the risk-averse decision maker, exporting may also serve as a strategy for overall risk reduction in any particular product line.

We have been arguing here that diverse foreign and domestic price movements are in large part the result of diverse underlying productivity patterns. The international diversity in levels and rates of growth in productivity are well documented (see Kravis (1976) and Hulten and

Nishimizu (1980)). Among the chief reasons for this diversity are differences in natural endowments, industrial relations, organizational structures, management techniques, methods of finance, as well as lags in the transfer of technology, shielding by patents, and divergences in government policies, regulatory constraints and business cycles. It follows that the firm can take advantage of the expected profit opportunities, as well as the expected risk reduction opportunities afforded by the remarkable diversity in international productivities by expanding into export markets.

It is important that export decisions be productivity based. This is particularly true if there is a significant lag between decision and implementation, and if such decisions are longer term in nature and are based on strategic marketing considerations. In these cases mere observation of existing international price differentials and ad hoc short term extrapolation of price trends will be inadequate. Underlying productivity trends will be essential elements in predicting longer term relative price movements. This requires the maintenance of productivity accounting systems, the study of trend and cyclical patterns of productivity changes in the product industries and underlying input industry, as well as the understanding of the input-output interrelations between the product industries and a sequence of input industries.

Export decisions involve, more often than not, significant investment in marketing and distribution. Such investments, as well as the overall risk reduction portfolio considerations, will often require longer term profitability considerations. It is in these situations that productivity based forecasting of relative price movements is likely to provide a larger margin of quality as compared with ordinary price forecasting. Estimates of underlying input requirements and total factor productivity trends provide the longer term relatively more stable fundamentals of the decision equation.

A diversification toward a mode of exporting n products to m markets affords a movement away from specific country risks associated with uncertainties about productivity differentials and eco-political developments. Whether any particular firm ought necessarily follow such a diversification path even if management is highly risk averse is open to question. International firms may find it advantageous to place greater emphasis on simultaneous diversification across country in one product or one product line. It is the former pattern of diversification that is extensively discussed in the literature concerning multinationals. In terms of our discussion here, with n possible products under consideration, there will be mn theoretically possible export-import projects. A simultaneous reduction in country-specific and product-specific risks can thus be achieved.

Obviously, portfolio diversification need not be conceptually a primary or even a very important force behind the growth of multinational operations, although some empirical evidence as to its role in the process is available (see Rugman (1980, Chapter 5), Rugman (1979, 1976), Severn (1974) and Cohen (1972)). Exploitation of comparative advantages among countries is likely to be a stronger, yet complementary model. After all, overall reduction in risk can be accomplished via investment in international securities without resorting to direct foreign investments. Nonetheless, both comparative advantage and risk reduction motives are directly related to productivity differential and therefore require productivity based analysis.

International diversification in production can extend along vertically integrated production processes, producing different components along the production line in different countries. For example, Ford's "world car" is also "worldly" in the literal sense that the parts and components that go into the final product are produced in at least ten countries. Differences in international productivity patterns ought to be an important factor behind moves toward international vertical diversification in production.

The Effects of Flexible Exchange Rates

During the transition from a regime of fixed exchange rates to a system of flexible exchange rates in the early seventies many international businessmen and bankers were apprehensive about the possible inhibiting effects of the risks associated with floating rates on the growth and development of international trade. As it turned out, such fears were exaggerated. Growth in international trade and multinational operations continued unabated. In fact, it can be reasonably argued that flexible exchange rates provided a stronger motivation for international diversification in production based in part on international differences in productivity patterns.

As illustrated by Branson (1975), under a regime of strictly fixed exchange rates national inflation rates will tend to converge to a world inflation rate. With the inflation transmission mechanisms generated under the system, individual countries with open economies are unable policywise to insulate their respective domestic price levels from the effects of changes in world prices. Under floating exchange rates domestic economic policies could gain a degree of freedom in terms of their divergent impact on domestic prices. Whether such insulating effects of domestic policies afforded by floating exchange rates are temporary or permanent is debatable. However, Kenen (1978) and Stern (1979) cite empirical evidence pointing to the power of domestic policies to insulate economies under flexible exchange rates from external price fluctuations.

In the context of our discussion, the insulating powers of domestic policies acquired under floating exchange rates preserve the rationale for international diversification of production as a risk reducing measure. Furthermore, with a degree of insulating from world inflation brought about by flexible exchange rates, differential patterns of productivities across countries will retain their important role both in the determination of comparative advantages and the estimation of risk reduction potential gained via international diversification. Thus, if anything, the transition from fixed to flexible exchange rates should have enhanced the growth of multinational enterprises by adding a risk reduction potential to other existing advantages inherent in international expansion of trade and production facilities. It is therefore hardly surprising that international trade and the relative contribution of multinationals continued to grow at a faster pace than domestic economic activities, regardless of the higher levels of uncertainty intuitively attributed to floating exchange rates. One may hypothesize that these intuitive perceptions gradually gave way to the realization that flexible exchange rates are likely to increase the magnitude of the divergence in price movements of individual products across countries, with differences in domestic policies and underlying productivity patterns being the major contributory factors.

Productivity Accounting Requirements and Their Use in Export Decisions

Much of the productivity information required for export decisions is contained in available standard cost accounting and budget data. Quantitative standards in effect target input requirements of the type specified in equations (7.3) through (7.9). Quantitative and price standards can be used to compute budgeted and/or projected average costs in accordance with (7.8). Comparisons between standard and actual productivities, as well as productivity variance analysis can be employed in the process of planning export decisions and their performance evaluation. Information from industry studies of historic productivity trends and cyclical behavior combined with inferences and estimates of quantitative and price standards of foreign competitors should provide the bulk of the relevant data base for export decisions. Thus, the productivity-based approach proposed in this paper relies mainly on a modified use of existing information and cost accounting systems. Nonetheless, input requirement standards for various capital inputs may be difficult to assess due to conceptual and data problems associated with the measurement of capital stocks and flows. These difficulties however are inescapable, and would have to be dealt with in any type of analytical decision making, domestic or international.

We shall now proceed with a retrospective analysis of a case study example illustrating the usefulness of productivity accounting in strategic export-import planning. In this case only partial information with regard to relative wages and relative labor productivities was generally available. Nevertheless it is shown that a productivity based analysis would have provided important insights.

Consider the relative output per man hour and labor cost patterns in the U.S. and Japan Iron and Steel Industries during the 1964–1973 period. Table 7-5 shows relative output per manhour, hourly labor costs, and unit labor cost indexes for Japan relative to the U.S. levels (U.S. = 100), computed for each year and translated to U.S. dollars using current and constant 1964 exchange rates. Suppose that prior to 1964 prospective Japanese steel exporters had at their disposal reasonably accurate forecasts along the lines of the data in table 7-5. How could this type of data help their strategic export planning? How could the same data have been used by U.S. steel executives in their long term production planning process?

A casual examination of the trends in table 7-5 reveals dramatic increases in Japanese relative to the U.S. productivity levels in steel and iron production as measured by output per manhour indexes. Japanese relative productivity in these industries increased from 1964 to 1973 by more than 250%. However, relative hourly labor costs in U.S. dollars at current exchange increased over the same period by roughly the same percentage. Hence, relative unit labor costs at current exchange rates hardly changed, with the increase in relative Japanese hourly labor costs almost exactly offsetting the cost advantage conferred by the relative productivity gains. It would appear upon a superficial examination of this data only, had it been available to decision makers in 1964 that no increased comparative advantage was in store for Japanese steel exports to the U.S. Clearly, such hypothetical 1964 productivity based analysis of export prospects to the U.S. (from a Japanese viewpoint) and competitive imports of steel (from the U.S. viewpoint) is, at best, incomplete. The role of other factors of production, primarily capital, has so far not been taken into account. Generally, statistics of capital stock and flow-of-capital services time series are more difficult but not impossible to compile. We know in retrospect that accurate forecasts of relative capital requirements in 1964 would have indicated that the introduction of the basic oxygen furnace technology in steel production in Japan would decrease significantly the relative capital to output ratios for the next decade. This impact, on top of little change in relative unit labor costs, was bound to create a significant comparative

Table 7-5. Relative Output per Hour, Hourly Labor Costs, and Unit Labor Costs in the Iron and Steel Industries: U.S. and Japan 1964-73

	Output per hour		*Hourly labor cost in U.S. dollars*				*Unit labor cost in U.S. dollars*			
			Constant 1964 exchange rates		*Current exchange rates*		*Constant 1964 exchange rates*		*Current exchange rates*	
	Minimum	*Maximum*	*Minimum*	*Maximum*	*Minimum*	*Maximum*	*Minimum*	*Maximum*	*Minimum*	*Maximum*
	United States									
Each Year	100	100	100	100	100	100	100	100	100	100
	Japan									
1964	43	54	17	17	17	17	31	40	31	40
1965	43	54	18	19	18	19	34	43	34	43
1966	51	63	20	20	20	20	31	39	31	39
1967	63	78	21	22	21	22	27	35	27	35
1968	68	85	23	24	23	24	27	35	28	35
1969	83	103	26	26	26	26	25	32	25	32
1970	97	120	30	30	30	30	25	31	25	32
1971	94	116	31	31	32	33	26	34	28	35
1972	102	127	30	30	36	37	24	30	29	36
1973	117	146	35	35	47	47	24	30	32	40

Source: Kendrick (1977) p. 62.
(U.S. = 100)

advantage in steel production for Japan over the U.S. This productivity based cost advantage may have been reinforced by the fact that the average rate of return throughout the period required by Japanese steel companies turned to be somewhat lower than the return on capital sought by their American counterparts.[7]

Whether Japanese steel executives actually engaged in the kind of productivity based export analysis described above is a matter of conjecture. The alternative hypothesis is that they decided on their level of exports to the U.S. during the late sixties and seventies on an ad hoc demand and supply basis. The latter hypothesis however seems unlikely. While the Japanese would have probably introduced the new technologies in order to cut costs even if exports prospects were less promising from a comparative advantage viewpoint, they would have planned on a significantly lower total volume of production for domestic markets only. The magnitude of the increase in Japanese steel exports that in fact took place would seem to have required substantial advance planning of higher levels of production capacity.[8] In the case of U.S. steel manufacturers it is known that no future oriented productivity based analytical efforts to anticipate the extent and degree of import competition ever took place during the sixties in any systematic manner. In fact, relatively little has been done in terms of large scale modernization of plant and introduction of new technologies during that period. Certainly, U.S. steel managers during the sixties and seventies turned out to be anything but long term profit maximizers. Explanations for their inefficient management of technology blame managerial myopia due to external pressures for short term profitability, excessive professional reliance on standard financial management techniques, depreciation rules which offered no incentive for large scale investments and replacements of plants, and little awareness of technological advances abroad and the potential domestic implications for profits of increased import competition. Whatever the reasons may be, subsequent developments in steel imports to the U.S. and their well known effects on prices, domestic employment levels, and protectionist responses, illustrates the importance of long term productivity based import-export analysis for planning and decision making purposes.

Interestingly, long term forecasts of productivity trends may be relatively easier than the forecasting of input prices and exchange rates. Input requirement predictions are derived from technological scenarios based on scientific and engineering assessments of technical feasibilities and derivative learning curves. The degree of uncertainty with respect to input quantity requirements per unit of output with specified characteristics diminishes significantly after the completion of the testing and pilot phases. The steel industry is again a case in point. Given the state of the art in the mid-sixties and the knowledge of impending technological advances, it would not have been too difficult to assess at that time the order of magnitude of productivity gains potentially obtainable by the introduction of the basic oxygen furnaces and continuous casting processes, as well as some other significant technological innovations. The principles governing these technologies were known well before their implementation. Even a crude translation of these technological estimates into input requirements and unit cost trends would have highlighted the prospects for fundamental changes in the structure of international steel production. Admittedly, relative changes in hourly labor compensation and exchange rates are more difficult to forecast in the long term. Yet, it would have been relatively safe to assume, in the case of steel in the mid sixties (as in the case of many other industries), that the magnitude of the changes in relative productivities would have overwhelmed the impact of forecast errors in other factors on unit costs.

During the 1981–82 world wide recession, steel companies in all steel producing countries including Japan experienced sharp reductions in output, declines in profitability and sizable excess capacity. Under these circumstances Japan's "Big Five" steel companies increased capital investment by more than 35% or $4.75 billion in the year ending March 31, 1983, with most of this investment directed toward energy efficient facilities and new steel product lines. These decisions were prompted by the anticipated need to match increasingly cost effective competition from Taiwan and South Korea, as well as by the necessity to adjusted to expected changes in steel use patterns. By contrast, U.S. steelmakers spent only $2.2 billion on capital investment during that same period and were continuously reducing their growth in capital spending throughout 1982.[9]

Observations partly similar to the steel industry case emerge from interesting case studies of export related policies pursued by Japanese firms in the color TV, computers and semiconductors industries. Tsurumi and Tsurumi (1980) point out that in the wake of the 1973–74 oil crisis "the Japanese color-TV set manufacturers made an effort to cut energy and production costs by simplifying the production processes by reducing the number of parts from 1,000–1,200 parts to 500–600 parts per set. This reduction was made possible by using the technology of semiconductors which reduced labor and other costs of production and also improved the quality of the color TV sets." (p. 593) The relative productivity advantages over U.S. competitors were achieved at a time when color TV sets reached the saturation level of their product life cycle—a stage when consumers demand became much more sensitive to price. This increased price sensitivity induced a pronounced shift in demand from console models which some large U.S. manufacturers such as Zenith and RCA were emphasizing to table and portable models on which the Japanese were concentrating their production. Thus, the failure of several big U.S. manufacturers of color TV sets to correctly anticipate a significant change in consumers preferences, coupled with their failure to complement in time new productivity augmenting technologies, resulted in sizable loss of their share of the U.S. market. That these technological and market opportunities were potentially foreseeable may be evidenced from the fact that a number of U.S. firms (e.g., Sears Roebuck and J.C. Penney) were already marketing at the time table and portable models mostly made in Japan.

As for the computers and semi-conductors industries, the Japanese government assisted initial development, as observed by Pugel et al. (1983), by subsidizing R&D and technology transfers and licensing. This enables some Japanese manufacturers to realize limited productivity and cost advantages related mainly to modes of utilization of skilled labor in certain hardware production phases. Yet Japanese firms in those industries had to offset technological lags and comparative weaknesses in software products and services relative to U.S. competitors in their thrust to capture significant shares of the U.S. and other foreign markets.

The engineering, economic, and accounting requirements for a long term productivity based assessment of trends in international competitiveness of a particular product can be better illustrated by outlining a heuristic sequence for such analysis:

(a) World-wide identification of major impending technological innovations at the time when they are beyond their basic research phase and well into their experimental development phase. Assessment of the technical and economic feasibility of these technologies, and forecast of their pace of implementation by prospective producers around the world.
(b) Translation of the technological forecasts in (a) into input requirement ratios (e.g., ratios of man hours to output, machine-hours to output, and materials to output.)
(c) Forecasts of long term gains in relative productivities based on (a) and (b) with emphasis on probabilities of maintaining and augmenting positive differentials in productivity levels and growth rates with respect to international competitors.
(d) Long term forecasts of trends in hourly labor compensation and in prices of pertinent materials, rents and services in the countries where large scale production of the product under consideration is anticipated. Forecasts in these trends could be based in part on forecasts of the respective rates of growth in national productivities, and the produc-

tivities of the underlying input industries in the countries under consideration.

(e) Forecasts of trends in the exchange rates of relevant currencies. These could be based in part on the forecasts of trends in the relative rates of growth in the national productivities in (d).

(f) Translation of the forecasts (b), (c), and (d) and (e) to predictions of relative changes in total costs per unit of output for any pair of countries. (Some of the end results of this analysis would be similar to the findings presented in table 7-1 of the Iron and Steel industries in Japan relative to the U.S., except that a much broader comparison of total costs per unit of output rather than labor unit cost only will be undertaken).

The information requirements for the sequence of forecasts outlined above are numerous. However, this type of analysis is necessary not only for systematic import-export and international production decision making, but also for the purpose of safeguarding competitiveness and domestic market shares. Comparative advantage forecasts of this kind, crude as they may be, are preferable to the absence of any systematic long term strategic planning in this area.

Conclusions

Comparative Productivity analysis is capable of making an important contribution toward improving the quality of export decisions. Productivity ratios or input requirements, along with input prices, are the most important determinants of actual and potential comparative advantages in international trade. Compared with changes in demand patterns, exchange rate fluctuations and relative input prices, relative productivity relationships are likely to be more stable and predictable, particularly in the long term. Underlying productivity trends reflect relative technological advantages which normally change at a much slower rate than market and monetary variables. Thus, while the role of exchange rates, input prices and demand elasticities are likely to be of major importance, it may be preferable in many instances to use relative productivities as a starting point for the analysis. This productivity data can be used for forecasts of long term gains in relative productivity and assessments of the chances of maintaining and augmenting positive differentials of levels and growth rates in productivity vis à vis competitors. In the absence of overall productivity advantages, export decisions relying solely on favorable market and exchange conditions are bound to be riskier, particularly for long term export entry and expansion decisions where significant investment commitments are called for. This type of productivity analysis is also likely to give firms important lead time for a possible change of course in their export policies since changes in relative technological trends, by being usually more gradual than relative changes in market prices, generally lend themselves to earlier and more accurate prediction. With the existence and order of magnitude of productivity advantages initially established, a sensitivity analysis of alternative monetary and market scenarios can provide the decision maker with indicators of the degree to which they are expected to counteract or reinforce comparative productivity advantages. Such productivity based foreknowledge is particularly acute in export strategies which require sizeable investments in marketing and distribution organizations.

Comparative productivity analysis draws upon information routinely compiled by corporate and national accounting systems. Quantitative standards and analysis of efficiency variances are an integral part of conventional standard cost accounting system, currently used by the majority of big and medium size U.S. manufacturing firms. National accounts include national, sectoral, and industry productivity figures, as well as input-output tables. Thus existing productivity accounting, usually contains, at the very least, information adequate for a crude comparative productivity analysis across international markets.

In this paper we have proposed the use of a simple micro-economic analytical framework for a systematic integration of relative productivity considerations into export decision systems. We have stated conditions for profitability which highlight the relationships between productivities, input prices and demand patterns under different market structures. It has been argued that dynamic input-output analysis based on data from successive input-output tables can provide us with a better understanding of the underlying causes of comparative cost advantages and thereby be potentially useful in strategic export decision. In olygopolistic markets conventional strategies may have to be supplemented not only by comparative productivity analysis, but also modified to allow for prospective politization of the market process. Finally, retrospective analysis of export planning of Japanese steel and iron to the U.S. and the response of U.S. companies provides a case study illustration of the potential importance of productivity accounting and productivity based analysis not only in export decisions, but also in general strategic planning oriented toward a world market view. This is reinforced by observations of case studies of export policies of Japanese firms in color TV sets, semi-conductors and computer industries.

Notes

1. Firm A may also produce for the domestic market. The impact of domestic production is subsumed in the elasticity of the average cost of export production ϕ_A.

2. Some of the X_i's represent flow of capital services, and their corresponding W_i's incorporate the user cost of capital.

3. If equations (7.5) and (7.6) do not hold then the cost advantage of Firm A over the representative B firm, as expressed in (7.8) does not guarantee profitability since B may simply be minimizing loss.

4. More precisely, ε_{AB} is dependent also on the level of P^{BB} and ε_{BB} is dependent, among other things, on the level of P^{AB}. Thus firm A cannot determine the price elasticity for its product in the B market without knowledge of the cost structure and demand conditions in B. The same holds for B.

5. A word of caution is appropriate in this context. Trade in intermediate or primary goods may occur between countries A and B, or between B and other countries, spurred, in part, by disparities in underlying productivities, which may affect the V_{ji}^{B}'s. In extreme cases, most intermediary or primary inputs may be imported to B from A or other countries. The comparative cost analysis based on succession of input-output tables may have to be modified accordingly.

6. Although Sraffa's system applies to a simple world without proprietary technologies serving as inputs, a dynamic input-output analysis based on sequences of changing input-output coefficients can incorporate effects of technical changes that have taken place in a succession of input industries.

7. A recent study of the competitiveness of the U.S. steel industry by Crandall (1981) emphasizes the disparities in hourly labor compensation *levels* between the U.S. and Japan. However, Crandall acknowledges the important role of changes in relative productivities generated by the diffusion of new technology, which aided the new steel exporters in competing with older established firms in the U.S. It is noteworthy that the Japanese gains in relative productivity contributed to reduction in the disparities in hourly compensation levels between the U.S. and Japan during the 1964–73 period as demonstrated by the trends in relative hourly labor compensation in table 7-1. Crandall also documents changes in raw material (ore) costs of the U.S. steel industry. Unfortunately comparable reliable data is not available for the Japanese steel industry to assess trends in relative costs. Nevertheless it seems unlikely that changes in U.S. domestic ore costs relative to world market prices played a very significant role in relative cost of production changes.

8. Production capacity planning in Japan may have been partly induced by governmental industrial policy. For discussion of the concept and practice of industrial policy see Lindbeck (1981). The Japanese government strategies of picking currently vulnerable future growth industries in which to make export market drives is well documented by Pugel et al. (1983) in their study of the Japanese semiconductors and computers industries. They point out that in the early 70's the Japanese government sheltered domestic markets in those industries by providing assistance through the availability of capital and R&D subsidization. This support became less significant as the companies and the industry became competitively viable. At the same time, Pugel et al note that the Japanese semiconductor industry has benefited from a shift in Japanese comparative advantages in favor of skilled labor intensive industries which appeared to offset their competitive weakness in the provision of software products.

9. See *Business Week*, June 13, 1983, No. 2794: 84–94, and June 27, 1983, No. 2796: 41–42.

8 PRODUCTIVITY BASED MANAGEMENT IN THE PUBLIC SECTOR AND IN REGULATED INDUSTRIES

The Valuation Problem

Most goods and services delivered by the public sector are not sold via the market place. In the absence of market transactions, the values of those services to recipients do not readily lend themselves to objective estimation. Hence, in the GNP accounts, the value of government services are stated at their cost. With government outputs measured by government inputs, productivity in government becomes stationary by definition. Accounting-wise, the efficiency of government operations is presumed never to improve or deteriorate. Conceptually, this macro-accounting treatment of government activity is neither realistic nor desirable, but it highlights the practical difficulties inherent in the measurement of nonmarketed services.

For our purposes, it is convenient to distinguish among three categories of government services: (a) nonmarketable services; (b) nonmarketed services; (c) marketed services. Nonmarketable services are primarily public goods (e.g., defense, law enforcement) which, by their nature, cannot be delivered to recipients via market sales. Consequently, while the quantity of such services can be crudely measured, their relative importance or utility to recipients cannot be objectively estimated in the absence of indicative market prices. Taxes cannot provide reasonable measures of value since individuals are coerced to pay them at specified legislated levels. Thus, the relative importance of nonmarketable services is in effect implicitly and subjectively weighted by the executive and the legislative branches of government. Nonmarketed services are mainly private goods (e.g., public education) which are supplied directly by the government to recipients rather than being sold by the public sector via the market. While their values may in some instances lend themselves to estimations based on prices of comparable services purchased in the market place (e.g., private education) the problems of inputing values to those services remain largely unresolved. This greatly complicates measurement of productivity levels and changes in the public sector. Even when government services are marketed (e.g., postal services) the problem of objectively estimating their value to recipients persists. While marketed government services may lend themselves to quantitative measures by the virtue of being sold, their prices are set by the government agencies, not by open market processes, and are therefore at best questionable indicators of value.

From the standpoint of productivity analysis, the valuation problems in the public sector translate into difficulties in assigning objective weights to public sector outputs, which, in turn, complicate measurement of productivity levels and changes in government enterprises and non-profit institutions. Yet, sound analyses of productivity in the public sector are extremely important; perhaps even more so than in the private sector. Most government agencies operate in noncompetitive environments immune from market penalties. Effective control over productivity performance and the design and maintenance of proper incentives for productivity improvements could provide safeguards for efficient operations in the public sector. This type of productivity based management and control call for reasonable and defensible measures of productivity in the provision of public sector services.

The productivity indexes discussed in chapter 2 will serve as a basis for our discussion here. In the first place, proper identification of output and input quantities $Y = \{Y_1, Y_2, \ldots, Y_i, \ldots, Y_m\}$ and $X = \{X_1, X_2, \ldots, X_i, \ldots, X_n\}$ always remains an essential requirement. This is often a very demanding yet inescapable task of management. Any major managerial decision making in the public or private sector involves either explicit or implicit recognition of inputs and outputs. What is often unique to the public sector is the valuation problem. Inputs, if purchased from outsiders, will have prices as indicators of value, but outputs will not since they are not sold to recipients. In a significant number of cases even inputs will not be obtained via market transactions (e.g., using the draft to recruit military personnel). Consequently, the problem of estimating the relative importance of each of the m outputs in total output, and each of the n inputs in total inputs without reliance on market prices has to be resolved.

Subjective Valuation

The relative importance of inputs and outputs in public sector production can be and usually is subjectively evaluated. In operational terms, it means that eqivalents to output prices $P = (P_1, P_2, \ldots, P_j, \ldots, P_m)$ and input prices $W = (W_2, W_2, \ldots, W_i, \ldots, W_n)$ have to subjectively be agreed upon by the decision-makers. This translates to assignment of subjective relative weights: $\beta_j = P_jY_j/\Sigma_jP_jY_j$ and $\alpha_i = W_iX_i/\Sigma_iW_iX_i$ which are respectively the public sector equivalents of the j-th output share in total revenue and i-th input share in total inputs. To underscore this equivalence we shall use the same notations α_i's and β_j's for private and public sector weights. Thus, once subjective weights are assigned, the productivity measurements developed in chapter 1 can be used to measure and analyze productivity in the public sector.

The equivalence between price based objective weights and subjective weights relies on the following rationale. The public sector equivalent of total revenue $\Sigma_jP_jY_j$ is the total value of all services delivered to recipients. The revenue realized by the j-th output in the private sector is translated to the value to recipients of the j-th government service. Thus, in analyzing public sector services $\beta_j = P_jY_j/\Sigma_jP_jY_j$ can be viewed as the share of the value of the j-th services out of total value of all services delivered. In this sense, the public sector equivalent of β_j represents the relative importance of the j-th service. An analogous interpretation can be offered for the public sector equivalents of the α_i's.

Alternatively, if Laspeyres or Paache type of indexes are used to measure productivity, subjective weights can be assigned to inputs and outputs in a similar manner. Note however that if total factor productivity (TFP) is measured by the index $\text{TFP} = \Sigma_jU_jY_j/\Sigma_iV_iX_i$ the subjective output weights (the U_j's) and the subjective input weights (the V_i's) have different market equivalents than their Divisia counterparts (the β_j's and α_i's). The market equivalent for U_j, the subjective weight assigned to the j-th output, is $\hat{P}_j$, a certain base price for the j-th output. Similarly, the market equivalent for V_i is $\hat{W}_i$, a certain base price for the i-th input.

Two points can be made in the defense of subjective valuation of the relative importance of inputs and outputs in the public sector. First, government officials are authorized constitutionally to make subjective judgments about relative importance of government services. Indeed, subjective decisions concerning the level and mix of government services are an integral part of the political process. Secondly, in the absence of objective indicators, subjective valuation becomes a prerequisite for governmental decision making. For purposes of clarity, consistency, coordination, accountability and control it is far better for such subjective valuation to be stated explicitly rather than being applied implicitly. Politically, however, explicit objective valuation may be difficult to attain. Introducing clarity into the vagueness of socio-economic and socio-political policymaking may make officials uncomfortably more observable and accountable to their constituencies and the public at large.

Objective Valuation and Relative Efficiency

Organizations often consist of subunits performing comparable tasks and thus using the same input types to deliver the same types of outputs. Examples of units performing activities so similar as to use the same type of resources to deliver the same type of services abound. Consider, for instance, elementary or secondary private schools, national parks, federal or state courts, the same class of navy destroyers or armoured divisions, to name only a few. Charnes, Cooper and Rhodes,[1] following Farrel's (1957) work, developed promising methods of objective valuation in analyzing relative efficiencies of comparable decision making units (DMUs). Specifically, they show that for comparable functions it is possible to obtain objective weights for indexes of relative efficiency in producing nonmarketable or nonmarketed services. This they accomplish via the use of mathematical programming techniques which allow each DMU to measure its efficiency relative to other comparable DMUs by using objectively derived input and output weights which happen to be the most favorable to its own relative efficiency rating.

Consider S comparable DMUs. The efficiency of the r-th DMU, TFP, is measured by the index $\text{TFP}_r = \Sigma_i U_j^r Y_j^r / \Sigma_i V_i^r X_i^r$ where the superscript $r(r = 1, \ldots, S)$ signifies that the pertinent input and output quantities and their respective weights relate to the rth DMU. Now, suppose we want to measure the relative efficiency of decision making unit indexed by number 2 $(r = 2)$. According to Charnes and Cooper, the problem of selecting the U_j and V_i weights in an objective manner is resolved by the following optimization:

$$\underset{U_j^2 V_i^2}{\text{MAX}} \ \text{TFP}_2 = \frac{\sum_j U_j^2 Y_j^2}{\sum_i V_i^2 X_i^2} \tag{8.1a}$$

subject to:

$$\frac{\sum_j U_j^2 Y_j^r}{\sum_j V_i^2 X_i^r} \leq 1 \qquad r = 1, 3, \ldots S \qquad (8.1b)$$

With all inputs and outputs known and measured DMU Number 2 chooses its weights U^2 and V^2 so as to maximize its TFP subject to the constraints that none of the other S-1 DMU can score a TFP higher than unity.[2] Since all inputs, outputs and their respective weights must be positive, then the constraints in (8.1b) imply that all DMU's are ranked from zero to unity. All relatively efficient DMUs score 1, and all DMU which score less than one are relatively inefficient.

Charnes and Cooper (1973) show that the functional maximization can be easily transformed into a linear programming problem which yields solutions for m weights for m outputs of DMU 2 (the U_j^2s) and n weights for n inputs of DMU 2 (the V_i^2s). Given the solutions for the weights, the total factor productivity ranking for DMU 2, TFP_2, which is consistent with maximization in (8.1a) and (8.1b) can be readily computed. This procedure can be repeated for all of the DMU's, in S, producing input and output weights and TFP rankings for each decision making unit. These TFP rankings are recorded on a zero-one interval scale. The distance of a particular DMU from unit measures the extent of its departure from relative efficiency.

Note that by the logic of the maximization process the weights determined for the TFP measurement of each particular DMU are the most favorable for its relative productivity score, given the input-output data constraints for the entire group of decision making units. Thus, managements of the DMUs whose efficiency is evaluated by their respective productivity scores should have fewer reasons to complain about the input and output weights assigned to them. These weights are objectively derived from the data, but at the same time are also skewed so as to give each of the ranked DMUs the best possible relative productivity performance score.

The TFP scores for all DMUs in S obtained via (8.1a) and (8.1b) will produce a subset of relatively efficient DMUs for which TFT $= 1$ and a subset of relatively inefficient DMUs for which TFP < 1. Assuming constant returns to scale, and scaling all TFPs so that they represent the input requirements for the same level of output, say $Y = 1$, the efficient DMUs can be viewed as being on the $Y = 1$ isoquant.

Assuming substitutibility of inputs, any linear combination of two efficient DMUs will be positioned on the isoquant. Thus, given linear production relationships, the distance between any inefficient DMU and the isoquant

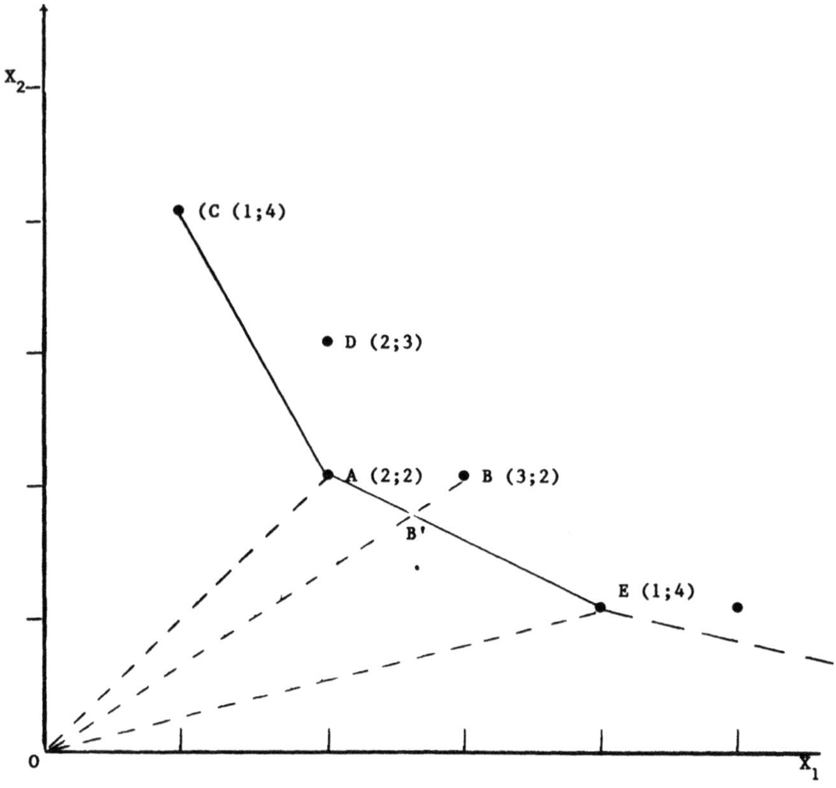

Figure 8-1. Efficient Points and Isoquant.

Source: Charnes et al. (1978 p. 436).

can be measured geometrically by a distance along a ray drawn from the origin between the inefficient DMU and isoquant (figure 8-1). This is easily understood by invoking Charnes and Cooper's own numerical illustration (See Charnes et al. (1978) pp. 436–437). Consider, for example, five decision making units *A, B, C, D* and *E*. Employing two inputs, X_1 and X_2, to produce one output Y. The input combinations required to produce one unit of output are given for each DMU as: $A(X_1 = 2,\ X_2 = 2)$; $B(X_1 = 3,\ X_2 = 2)$; $C(X_1 = 1,\ X_2 = 4)$; $D(X_1 = 2,\ X_2 = 3)$; $E(X_1 = 1,\ X_2 = 4)$. Obviously, *B* and *D* are inefficient relative to *A*. Decisions making units *A, C* and *E* will score as relatively efficient (i.e., $TFP_A = TFP_C = TFP_E = 1$).

Focusing on the measurement of *B*'s efficiency we maximize TFP_B subject to the constraints that none of the other DMU's productivity ratings can exceed unity. Solving, in accordance with (8.1a) and (8.1b) we obtain the most favorable input weights for *B* of $V_1^B = 1/6$; $V_2^B = 1/3$. Applying these weights, we get relative efficiency scoring for decision making unit *B* of $TFP_B = 6/7$, which means that only 6/7 of the amount of each input employed by DMU *B* should have been efficiently used to produce each unit of output. Alternatively, $TFP_B = 6/7$ indicates that by the standard of the relative efficiency of DMUs *A* and *C*, unit *B* should have produced 7/6 units of output rather than the one unit of output actually delivered. Geometrically, $\overline{CAE}$ (in figure 8-1) is the unit isoquant, determined by the linear combinations of the relatively efficient DMUs. *B*, by being outside the isoquant, is relatively inefficient. A movement along the ray *OB'B* from *B* to *B'* would require the production of one unit with 6/7 of the amount of each of the inputs. These savings in input, if accomplished, would have made DMU *B* relatively efficient by placing it on the unit isoquant.

Precisely the same procedure can be applied to rank the relative efficiency of DMU *D*. In the process, parts of the entire production function surface are constructed. In this particular example, $\overline{CA}$ and $\overline{AE}$ are the pertinent parts of the production function in the sense that they represent the loci of the relatively efficient combinations of inputs X_1 and X_2 required to produce one unit of output *Y*. Consequently, this method enables us to deduce a relative efficiency frontier. Ideally, estimation of an absolute efficiency frontier reflecting efficient technology or state of the art would be preferable. Unfortunately, one cannot derive such absolute frontiers from empirical data unless one is prepared to assume a priori that all empirical observations are efficient, which assumes away inefficiencies and negates the managerial need for productivity analysis. Thus, absolute efficiency frontiers can be estimated in a reasonable manner only for very specific production processes reflecting reliable technical engineering assessments of the state of the art. These are practically impossible for aggregate production processes in private and public sectors for which no technical state of the art knowledge, independent of empirical observations, exists. Thus estimation of relative efficiency frontiers from actual data may be the best we can hope for in most cases.

Data Envelopment Analysis

The relative efficiency ranking methods developed so far using either subjective or objective weights, enable management to rank DMUs in accordance with their relative efficiencies or productivities. The comparative

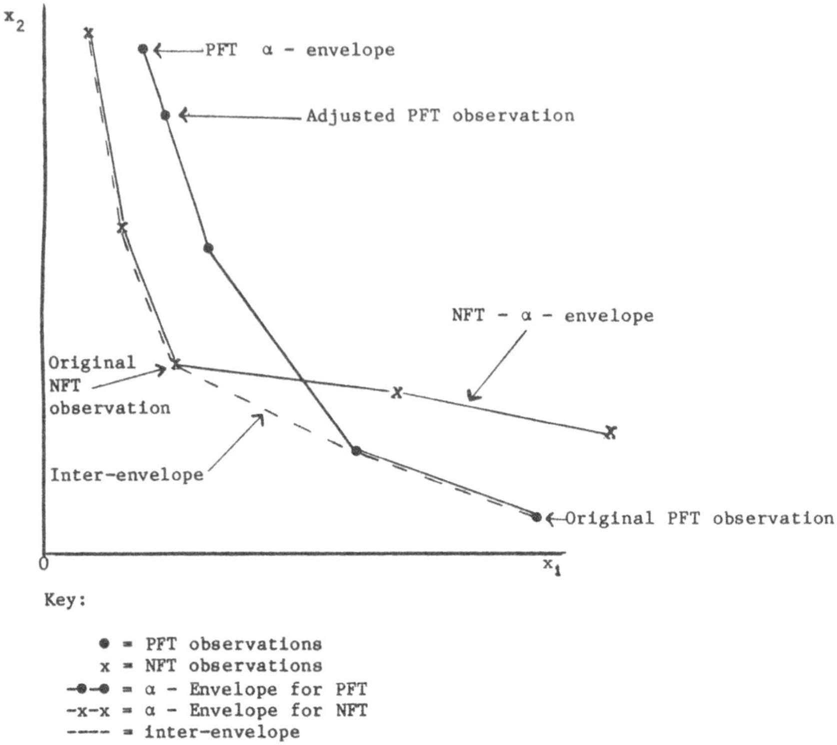

Figure 8-2. Data Envelopment Analysis.

Source: Charnes and Cooper (1980 p. 157).

objective weighting method, as developed by Charnes and Cooper and their colleagues, also provides managers with relative efficiency frontiers. This line of reasoning is expanded further by Charnes et al. (1978, pp. 150–159). Suppose we have comparable Decision Making Units operating in different environments (i.e., different organizations or different programs). For example, suppose that comparable schools with the same type of inputs and outputs operate under two different educational approaches denoted as Program I and Program II.[3] Using the procedure in (8.1a) and (8.1b) we can obtain the productivity rankings and the efficiency frontiers of DMUs in Program I and Program II. By doing so let us suppose that we obtain the unit isoquants for Program I and Program II, which happen to intersect each other (see figure 8-2). This means that Program I is more efficient in the region to the right where relatively less of input X_2 is used and relatively more of input X_1 is used, while Program II is more efficient in the region to the left where relatively less of input X_1 is used and relatively more input X_2 is used. The unit isoquants of the two programs are often referred to as envelope I and envelope II since they "envelope" the empirical observations of their respective DMUs by relative efficiency frontiers.

The comparisons between program I and program II provide us with the possibility to differentiate between the concepts of *managerial efficiency* and *program efficiency*. Within each program, managerial efficiency is rated by the positions of each DMU relative to its own efficiency frontier envelope. Program efficiency evaluates the efficiency of program I relative to program II regardless of the degrees of managerial inefficiencies present in each of the programs. To that end, we assume that all DMUs in programs I and II are efficient and proceed to adjust the relatively inefficient DMUs so as to bring them to the unit isoquant. This can be done by equiproportionally scaling down the input requirements of the relatively inefficient DMUs. In the numerical example of Charnes et al. (1978) this process would mean, for example, the adjustment of the relatively inefficient DMU B from B to B' by equiproportionally scaling down its inputs X_1 and X_2 by a factor of 6/7. Once all DMUs are placed on their respective efficiency frontier envelopes and the managerial inefficiencies within the respective programs eliminated comparisons of program efficiencies are facilitated. One possibility is to apply the maximization procedure in (8.1a) and (8.1b) to the entire set of adjusted DMUs to produce an overall data envelopment. The results are illustrated in figure 8-2.

Where portions of the original efficiency frontier envelopes of each program, together with an interenvelope portion, form the *overall* relative efficiency frontiers. In this particular illustration, the overall data envelope consists of a portion of Program I envelope for input combinations for which it is relatively more efficient (high levels of X_1 and low levels of X_2) as well as a portion of Program II envelope for inputs combinations for which Program II is relatively efficient. The interenvelope portion is an improvement, within a particular range of input combinations, over the efficiency of both programs.

Relative Efficiency Analysis in Education: A Case Study (Charnes and Cooper (1980))

Charnes and Cooper (1980, pp. 151–159) reported on an interesting application of their data envelopment analysis to assess program efficiencies and managerial efficiencies in an experimental educational project. The illustration below is based on data from "Program Follow-Through," a large-scale experiment in U.S. public school education designed to help disadvantaged children. This educational experiment was carried out at 70 selected school sites in various parts of the U.S.A. Assessment of this project was done on the basis of observations from Program Follow Through (PFT) and from Non-Follow-Through (NFT) sites. For purposes of efficiency evaluation of terminal (grade 3) results, the following three outputs and five inputs were chosen.

Outputs:

Y_1 Total reading score as measured by the Metropolitan Achievement Test.

Y_2 Total mathematics score as measured by the Metropolitan Achievement Test.

Y_3 Coopersmith Self-Esteem Inventory, intended as a measure of self-esteem.

Inputs:

X_1 Education level of mother as measured in terms of percentage of high school graduates among female parents.

X_2 Highest occupation of family member according to a prearranged rating scale.

X_3 Parental visit index representing the number of visits to the school site or with Follow-Through personnel.

X_4 Parent counseling index calculated from data on time spent with children on school related topics such as reading together etc.

X_5 Number of teachers at a given PFT or NFT site.

Relative TFP measures were computed for all PFT and NFP sites in accordance with (8.1a) and (8.1b), with the results shown in table 8-1. The relatively efficient sites in the PFT and NFP sets (i.e., the sites that scored a TFP value of 1) generated the respective PFT and NFP envelopes or efficiency frontiers. The differences between the proportion of sites that achieved TFP values of unity in the PFT and NPF programs were found to be statistically not significant at the .05 level. It was therefore possible to infer that managers in the two programs, PFT and NFP, had about equal likelihood of being on their respective program-referenced efficiency fron-

Table 8-1. PFT and NFT Program-Specific α-Envelope Efficiency Values

PFT Site No.	*Relative Efficiency Value*	*NFT Site No.*	*Relative Efficiency Value*
1*	1.00	50	0.95
2	0.90	51	0.92
3	0.98	52*	1.00
4	0.90	53	0.87
5*	1.00	54*	1.00
6	0.90	55*	1.00
7	0.89	56*	1.00
8	0.91	57	0.92
9	0.87	58*	1.00
10*	1.00	59	0.92
11	0.98	60	0.98
12	0.97	61	0.88
13	0.86	62*	1.00
14	0.98	63	0.96
15*	1.00	64	0.91
16	0.95	65	0.97
17*	1.00	66	0.92
18*	1.00	67	0.92
19	0.95	68*	1.00
20*	1.00	69*	1.00
21*	1.00	70	0.94
22*	1.00		
23	0.96		
24*	1.00		
25	0.97		
26	0.93		
27*	1.00		
28	0.94		
29	0.84		
30	0.90		
31	0.83		
32	0.90		
33	0.94		
34	0.85		
35*	1.00		
36	0.80		
37	0.94		
38	0.94		
39	0.91		

(continued on next page)

Table 8-1. *(continued)*

PFT Site No.	*Relative Efficiency Value*	*NFT Site No.*	*Relative Efficiency Value*
40*	1.00		
41	0.94		
42	0.94		
43	0.87		
44*	1.00		
45	0.89		
46	0.90		
47*	1.00		
48*	1.00		
49*	1.00		

*Denotes a site with an efficiency value of "1".
Source: Charnes and Cooper (1980) p. 156.

tiers. These findings imply that there is little, if any, reason to believe that Project Follow Through enables or induces more of its managers to operate efficiently within the limits of their program constraints as compared with managers of sites that did not undertake Project Follow Through. However, these calculations do not address differences between the distribution values of efficiency in the two programs. Only managerial efficiencies within PFT and NPF were analyzed. Program efficiencies were not evaluated on a comparative basis.

For direct comparisons between the efficiencies of the two programs Charnes and Cooper proceeded to compute the interenvelope efficiency values in the manner discussed above. The results are shown in table 8-2. Now it is assumed that all managers of all sites are operating efficiently. All TFP values lower than unity are attributable solely to the differential impact of PFT or NFT program constraints. Using the Kullback-Leiber statistics, Charnes and Cooper find that PFT observations, taken all together, are more distant from the interenvelope than is the case for the distribution of the NFT observations. Thus, an important preliminary conclusion drawn from this analysis is that Project Follow Through does not pass the relative efficiency test when compared with performances of comparable units that did not participate in this project.

The findings of the data envelopement analysis do not necessarily suggest that Project Follow Through should have been discontinued on grounds of

Table 8-2. Inter-Envelope Efficiency Values

PFT In	h_0* *Value*	*NFT No.*	h_0* *Value*
1	0.92	50*	1.00
2*	1.00	51*	1.00
3*	0.94	52*	1.00
4*	1.00	53*	1.00
5	0.93	54*	1.00
6*	1.00	55	0.99
7	0.99	56*	1.00
8*	1.00	57*	1.00
9	0.98	58*	1.00
10	0.92	59*	1.00
11*	1.00	60*	1.00
12*	1.00	61*	1.00
13	0.99	62*	1.00
14	0.95	63*	1.00
15*	1.00	64*	1.00
16*	1.00	65*	1.00
17*	1.00	66*	1.00
18*	1.00	67*	1.00
19	0.99	68	0.99
20*	1.00	69*	1.00
21*	1.00	70*	1.00
22*	0.99		
23	1.00		
24*	1.00		
25*	1.00		
26	0.99		
27*	1.00		
28*	1.00		
29	0.99		
30*	1.00		
31	0.99		
32*	1.00		
33	0.99		
34	0.98		
35*	1.00		
36*	1.00		
37*	0.94		
38	0.99		
39*	1.00		

(continued on next page)

Table 8-2. *(continued)*

PFT In	h_0* *Value*	*NFT No.*	h_0* *Value*
40	0.95		
41	0.99		
42*	1.00		
43	0.99		
44*	1.00		
45	0.99		
46*	1.00		
47*	1.00		
48*	1.00		
49*	1.00		

*Denotes a site with an efficiency value of "1".
Source: Charnes and Cooper (1980) p. 157.

inefficiency. They do indicate however that as implemented at the time, PFT did not appear to deliver superior results. A reevaluation of the project may be called for. It could not be ruled out that upon reexamination, different implementation strategies may be found so as to improve the PFT program efficiency. Relative efficiency boundaries do not represent absolute state of the art frontiers and ought not be viewed as measures of the total potentials of evaluated programs.

The Role of Productivity in Rate of Return Regulation

Kendrick (1975) and Sudit (1979) proposed alternative models of indexed pricing of services, incorporating total factor productivity and cost saving incentives in the framework of rate of return regulation. Sinden (1980) discusses various models which might be used to determine how the productivity gains might be shared by the firm and the consumer once a rate adjustment formula based on productivity has been agreed upon. Chandry and Sudit (1982) broaden these models by: (a) building efficiency and profit incentives directly into the allowed rate of return formulae to strengthen performance incentives; (b) incorporating measures of the effectiveness of rate making relative to multiple regulatory goals (e.g., quality, fairness) and built-in incentives for improving effectiveness; (c) advocating complete freedom for the regulated firm in pricing individual services, subject to an overall constraint in weighted average rate changes, to improve efficiency in pricing; (d) recommending the use of capital measures unadjusted for rates of utilization in computing total factor productivity to minimize allocative inefficiencies. Within this extended frame of reference, new total factor productivity data are presented to illustrate use of the proposed interim productivity based rate adjustment clause and alternative effectiveness measurements and controls are discussed.

In this section we discuss some of the recent developments in productivity based management in rate of return regulation. We follow with minor modifications the framework developed by Chaudry and Sudit (1982), while evaluating some of the earlier contributions to productivity based regulatory management.

Indexed pricing schemes and automatic rate adjustment clauses are not new. Lindsay (1977) and Schmidt (1980) provide good discussions of their history. Scott (1980) presents a comprehensive analysis of the effects of fuel cost adjustments for electric utilities. Productivity based rate adjustment clauses have been proposed and/or implemented mostly, if not exclusively, in telecommunications. The New Jersey and Michigan Bell experiences under these clauses, as well as the Illinois Bell proposal are discussed in detail by Latimer (1974), Kendrick (1975), Sudit (1979) and Schmidt (1980). Of course the wider problems associated with a variety of inefficiencies inherent in rate of return regulation as it is practiced have been a subject of numerous studies. Among recent interesting contributions to analysis and discussion, to mention only a few, are Baron (1980a, 1980b) Sherman (1980, 1977), Vogelsang and Finsinger (1979) and Arzac and Edwards (1979).

Chaudry and Sudit (1982) formulate a simple behavioral model which is designed to capture the essentials of rate of return regulation as it is currently practiced in the U.S. Following this approach we do not assume that regulatory agencies attempt to maximize social welfare functions, either global or partial. Likewise, regulated firms are not assumed necessarily to maximize profits, minimize costs, or even operate on technically efficient frontiers. We argue that in real world settings judicious productivity based management on behalf of regulatory agencies and regulated firms has the potential of improving the economic well-being of customers, shareholders and employees.

Consider a regulatory commission which sets the rates $\boldsymbol{P} = (P_1, P_2, \ldots, P_j, \ldots, P_m)$ for m services so as to reflect the basic interests of customers and of those services, as well as the interests of the shareholders, bondholders and employees of the regulated firms. Under rate of return regulation the task of the regulator can be stated as follows:

$$\text{Set } \boldsymbol{P} = (P_1, \mathrm{P}_2, \ldots P_j \ldots P_m) \tag{8.2a}$$

subject to:

$$Z \leq r = \left\{ \frac{\sum_{j=1}^{m} P_j Y_j - \sum_{i=1}^{n} W_i X_i}{K} \right\} \leq S \tag{8.2b}$$

where Y_j is the quantity of the j-th service, X_i and W_i are respectively the quantity and price of the i-th input, K is the stock of capital, r is the actual rate of return, and S is the maximum allowed rate of return. Z is a minimum cost of capital below which the return to investors, as compared with alternative opportunities at comparable degrees of risk, will be eroded.

The regulatory agency periodically sets new rates, $\boldsymbol{P}$, within the rate of return constraint. The regulated firm may initiate rate proceedings if it perceives r to fall below Z in (8.2b). The commission will consider the request to increase rates to protect the interests of investors and employees, and to preserve the economic viability of the firm. It sets a maximum allowed rate of return, S, to protect the customers from excessively high monopoly prices, and presumably society from monopoly welfare losses. By keeping S and thereby P as low as possible, without endangering the provision of services or their quality, the regulatory agency could be viewed as moving in the direction of maximizing consumers' surplus subject to operational constraints.

Among the latter, preservation of quality of service is important. For example, one key quality parameter may be the reliability of service, which means that production capacity would be sufficient to meet the anticipated demand. Since it is possible to increase profitability or to keep rates low at the expense of service quality, safeguarding minimal quality standards is designed to protect the interests of the consumers.

In theory, the commission sets and leaves the determination rates to the discretion of the regulation company. In practice, the freedom of the firm to set rates for specific services is subject to regulatory review and is often constrained by subsidiary objectives of the regulators intended to protect interests of specific customer groups and to ensure that quality of service is maintained. Input prices and quantity requirements are also subject to regulatory review, with the commission empowered to disallow costs which are deemed excessive or unjustified, thereby affecting S and $\boldsymbol{P}$.

To establish the relationship between changes in unit costs, rates and productivity over time we rearrange the rate of return expression in (8.2b):

$$\sum_{j=1}^{m} \dot{P}_j Y_j = \sum_{j=1}^{n} W_j X_j + (Z + \pi) K \tag{8.3}$$

where $\pi = r - Z$ is the above-normal rate of return on capital.

Differentiating (8.3) with respect to time and rearranging we obtain:

$$\sum_{j=1}^{m} \frac{\dot{P}_j}{P_j} \beta_j = \sum_{j=1}^{n} \frac{\dot{W}_j}{W_j} \alpha_j + \frac{\dot{Z}}{Z} \alpha_K - \frac{\dot{\text{TFP}}}{\text{TFP}} + \frac{\dot{\pi}}{\pi} \gamma_K + \frac{\dot{K}}{K} \gamma_K \tag{8.4}$$

where:

$$\beta_j = \frac{P_j Y_j}{\sum_{j=1}^{m} P_j Y_j} \; ; \; \alpha_j = \frac{W_i X_i}{\sum_{j=1}^{n} P_j Y_j} \text{ and } \alpha_K = \frac{ZK}{\sum_{j=1}^{m} P_j Y_j}$$

are respectively the shares of revenues generated by the j-th output, total factor costs incurred by the i-th inputs and total costs incurred by capital out of total revenues.

$$\gamma_K = \frac{\pi}{\sum_{j=1}^{m} P_j Y_j}$$

is the share of above normal profits out of total revenues.

$$\frac{\dot{\text{TFP}}}{\text{TFP}} = \sum_{j=1}^{n} \frac{\dot{Y}_j}{Y_j} \beta_j - \sum_{i=1}^{n} \frac{\dot{X}_j}{X_j} \alpha_j - \frac{\dot{K}}{K} \alpha_K - \frac{\dot{K}}{K} \gamma_K$$

is the percent change in total factor productivity (TFP), stated as the difference between the weighted percent changes in outputs and inputs. The weights applied to the percent changes in outputs and inputs in the productivity formula are their respective revenue shares, as defined above. The use of revenue shares instead of cost shares is designed to preserve path independence of the Divisia TFP index in the case of nonconstant returns to scale in production (see Hulten (1973) and Nadiri and Schankerman (1980)).

To better understand the cost-productivity relationship in equation (8.4) let us assume what will be traditionally conceived as perfect regulation: The commission *always* sets the maximum allowed rate of return, S, precisely equal to the cost of capital Z. The regulated company manages to obtain an actual rate of return exactly equal to the allowed one. Consequently, $r = Z = S$ and $\pi = 0$. $\pi = o$ implies $\gamma_K = 0$. The expression in (8.4) reduces to:

$$\sum_{j=1}^{m} \frac{\dot{P}_j}{P_j} \beta_j = \sum_{i=1}^{n} \frac{\dot{W}_j}{W_j} \alpha_j + \frac{\dot{Z}}{Z} \alpha_K - \frac{\dot{\text{TFP}}}{\text{TFP}} \tag{8.5}$$

According to (8.5), the regulator will let the weighted sum of the percent changes in rates equal the difference between the sum of the weighted changes in input prices and changes in total factor productivity (with the levels and changes in the actual rate of return of the firm held equal to the corresponding levels and changes in the cost of capital of the firm).

Under the present system of regulation, rates are allowed to change periodically following hearing and proceedings. In between regulatory proceedings, rates remain unchanged (i.e., $\Sigma_{j=1}^{m}(\dot{P}_j/P_j)\beta_j = 0$). Consequently, in the absence of regulatory action, the system will be in steady state only so long as productivity advances fully offset increases in input prices; otherwise, the constraint in (8.2b) will be violated and regulatory intervention to either increase or decrease rates will be called for. However, it is important to realize that even in a steady state environment there is little if any incentive under the present regulatory system for regulated firms to improve their productivity performance. Thorough and continuous regulatory auditing of efficiency of operations is likely to be either ineffective or costly. Hence, the need for built-in productivity incentives.

It is also evident from the cost-productivity relationships in (8.4) that in inflationary times when productivity advances lag significantly behind increases in input prices the frequency of rate proceedings will rise. Between regulatory rate decisions, the system will be in a state of disequilibrium. The effects of continuous regulatory lags over long periods of continuously high inflation are a matter of some controversy. Baumol (1970) viewed regulatory lags as providing efficiency incentives by motivating regulated firms to increase productivity in order to minimize the erosion of earnings between regulatory proceedings. But in reality, the "make-whole mentality" prevents such gains from being realized because there is a tendency to push costs up just before going into a rate case. Thus the regulatory lag provides only a short term incentive, if any. In addition, whenever uncontrollable inflationary increases in input prices exceeding productivity gains by a significant order of magnitude, the potential rewards to reasonable improvements in the rate of productivity growth are likely to be perceived as relatively small. Thus, in the absence of some interim relief, planned investment programs may have to be delayed or existing programs may have to be discontinued.

Productivity Based Rate Adjustment Clauses

Based on the productivity-cost relationship discussed above, Chaudry and Sudit (1982) propose a Comprehensive Interim Productivity Based Rate Adjustment Clause (CIPRAC) which incorporates: (a) built-in productivity incentives; (b) built-in input cost saving incentives; and (c) built-in profit incentives. Using the productivity-cost relationship in (8.4) this interim rate adjustment clause takes the following form:

$$\left[\sum_{j=1}^{m} \frac{\dot{P}_j}{P_j} \beta_j\right]^A = \sum_{i=1}^{n} \left[\frac{\dot{W}_j}{W_j}\right]^{\text{Std.}} \alpha_j + \left[\frac{\dot{Z}}{Z}\right]^{\text{Std.}} \alpha_K - \left[\frac{\dot{\text{TFP}}}{\text{TFP}}\right]^{\text{Std}} \tag{8.6}$$

subject to:

$$Z \leq r \leq S + \delta \left[\frac{\dot{\text{TFP}}}{\text{TFP}} - \left(\frac{\dot{\text{TFP}}}{\text{TFP}}\right)^{\text{Std.}} + \mu \left[\left(\frac{\dot{W}}{W}\right)^{\text{Std.}} - \frac{\dot{W}}{W}\right]\right. \tag{8.6a}$$

where $0 \leq \delta \leq 1$; and $0 \leq \mu \leq 1$. $[\dot{W}/W]^{Std.}$ is the standard for the change in unit price of the i-th input; $[\dot{Z}/Z]^{Std.}$ is the standard for the change in the opportunity cost of capital; and $[\dot{TFP}/TFP]^{Std.}$ is the standard set for productivity growth. $[\Sigma_{j=1}^{m}(\dot{P}_j/P_j)\beta_j]^A$ is the weighted sum of rate changes allowed by the adjustment clause. The superscript *Std.* denotes a standard set by the commission, and the superscript *A* denotes the adjustment allowed by the clause in 8.6. δ and μ are profit-related incentive parameters pertaining to productivity and costs.

The constraint in (8.6a) provides a way for making adjustments to the current level of the allowed rate of return S. The adjustments could depend on the cost and productivity performance of the firm, relative to the respective standards. The cost standards and productivity standards, as well as the incentive parameters δ and μ are to be set by the regulators who would take quality and reliability of service into account in setting and periodically reviewing these standards and parameters. The allowed rate of return, S, is set by the commission in the course of conventional rate of return proceedings. In the interim periods between rate proceedings, rates are adjusted periodically, say on quarterly or annual basis according to the formula in (8.6). If and when, despite the interim adjustments, the rate of return constraint is violated, either the regulator or the firm may initiate full fledged hearings. The use of CIPRAC need not involve the Commission in determining the rate structure. The firm could be allowed to set individual rates subject to the proviso that no cross-subsidy is involved. This rate structuring freedom, in conjunction with the built-in productivity incentives, is likely to enhance pricing efficiency.

Productivity Incentives

Standards for target productivity performance $[\dot{TFP}/TFP]^{Std.}$ are set and monitored by the commission. These standards can be determined through formal regulatory proceedings and will be based on historical trends in productivity performance by the regulated firm, productivity growth records in the industry and related industries, cyclical factors and special circumstances expected to confront the company. If the actual productivity improvement by the company exceeds the standard it will be allowed to convert a portion of it to higher earnings via the rate adjustment in (8.6) and subject to the constraint in (8.6a). Hence, the built-in incentive to increase productivity.

However the CIPRAC formula in (8.6) is a two way adjustment clause. Consequently, if actual productivity growth realized by the company falls below standard (a five year moving average), the company would be penalized by lower earnings via application of the higher productivity standard in the rate adjustment formula. If the shortfall is of sufficient magnitude to cause the actual rate of return r to fall below the cost of capital, the firm may request regulatory action to increase rates. However, in the course of justifying its request for rate increases beyond the period increases mandated by the formula, the firm will have to explain in detail its deficient productivity performance. If however poor productivity performance persists, the constraint in (8.6a) would suggest an adjustment in the allowed rate of return, unless the firm is able to keep its input price increases sufficiently below the standard.

It is preferable that the capital stock measure used in CIPRAC for the computation of total factor productivity not be adjusted for capacity utilization. This provides a built-in disincentive for unproductive overbuilding or gold plating of plant which would depress actual productivity performance by inflating the growth in its capital input without generating corresponding increases in output. Moreover, for the very same reasons, the incorporation of unutilized capital in TFP measures is likely to attenuate or counteract Averch-Johnson type of incentive to over-capitalize. This approach is also important in view of the fact that our rate adjustment clause allows for the possibility that the allowed rate of return will be adjusted above the cost of capital level to provide profit incentives as defined in (8.6a).

Built-In Cost Efficiency Incentives

Cost efficiency incentives are incorporated into the CIPRAC formula by making the allowed rate changes $[\Sigma_{j=1}^{m}(\dot{P}_j/P_j)\beta_j]^A$ a function of standard changes in input prices $[\dot{W}_i/W_i]^{\text{Std.}}$ rather than the actual changes $[\dot{W}_i/W_i]$ for $i = 1, \ldots, n$. The standards for changes in wages, fringe benefits and prices of materials, rents and services purchased from outside suppliers can be determined by using exogenous market references for the same or comparable inputs. If the regulated firm succeeds in economizing on input prices by keeping their increases below the corresponding increases in the market reference standards of these inputs, it will be rewarded by being allowed to keep a portion of these savings as increased earnings via (8.6) and (8.6a). By the same procedure, the firm will be penalized earningwise for a failure to keep input prices it pays at or below market levels. Hence, the incentive to economize on input costs.

In conventional regulatory proceedings, cost control is exercised through cost audits by the regulators. In practice, cost information is asymmetric and commission staffs often lack the resources and time to acquire information adequate for effective examination and audit of the reliability and reasonableness of company figures. Thus, built-in cost incentives, of the type proposed in (8.6) can provide an important supplementary instrument in promoting effective cost management.

The determination of the standard for cost of capital changes $[\dot{Z}/Z]^{Std.}$ in (8.6) requires some elaboration. The procedures commonly employed by commissions to determine the cost of capital for the regulated firm are described by Robichek (1980). The regulator usually seeks expert testimony on the cost of equity and weighs the cost of equity and embedded debt by the respective *actual* share of total book value of equity and debt funds in total obligations. Sherman (1977) has shown that this procedure may motivate strategic behavior on the part of the firm by providing it with the incentive to manipulate its equity component if it anticipates that the allowed rate of return S will be set at a margin above its perceived cost of capital Z, as usually would be the case following the procedure in (8.6a). To attenuate this problem, Chaudry and Sudit (1982) recommend that, in setting $Z^{Std.}$ and $[\dot{Z}/Z]^{Std.}$ the commissions follow the practice outlined in Baron (1980) and Nichols (1955). Cost of capital standards should be set on the basis of a comparable earnings on debt and equity. Since, the determination of the standard cost of capital will depend on exogenous factors only, the process will attenuate incentives for strategic behavior.

Built-in Rate of Return Incentives

The problems arising from the lack of effective built-in profit incentives in the rate of return mechanism are aptly summarized by Sherman (1980, p. 11): "Even if management of this regulated firm is faithful to the shareholders' interest in profit, there is still a problem of efficiency under rate of return regulation: whereas the ordinary firm seeks only profit, the rate-of-return regulated firm has two goals. One goal is to earn profit and the other is to be allowed to keep it." The built-in rate of return incentives in 8.6a are designed to allow the regulated company to keep a portion of the above normal profits it earned by productivity and cost performances which exceed exogenous standards for these areas and to lose those resulting from performance that falls short of these standards.

The incentive coefficients δ and μ, used to reflect the relative importance of the incentives in the rate of return constraint, are determined by the regulator subject to presentations and arguments of all parties to the regulatory process. The agreed upon levels of these parameters in conjunction with the productivity and other standards involved in the process will determine the strength of the respective incentives. The impact of these incentives on the upper limit of the constraint (8.6a) is *not* cumulative (as is apparent from the formula). In other words, the performance rewards or penalties will change the ceiling for r only for the adjustment period in question. For the next adjustment period the base level of the upper limit in (8.6a) will be the allowed rate of return S determined during the preceding full-fledged rate-of-return proceedings. This will avert any perpetuation of rewards or penalties, which would be unfair and could seriously interfere with the maintenance of effective efficiency, cost and quality incentives.

In order to motivate management to respond to the profit incentive it may be desirable to supplement CIPRAC with a profit sharing plan, depending upon the specific circumstances of the firm. The surplus profits that the regulated firm is allowed to keep as a reward for above-standard performance.

$$K\delta\left[\frac{\dot{\mathrm{TFP}}}{\mathrm{TFP}} - \left(\frac{\dot{\mathrm{TFP}}}{\mathrm{TFP}}\right)^{\mathrm{Std.}}\right] + K\mu\left[\left(\frac{\dot{W}}{W}\right)^{\mathrm{Std.}} + \frac{\dot{W}_i}{W_i}\right] \tag{8.7}$$

could be distributed in such a way as to help maintain and to further improve good performance.

The incentive parameters, δ and μ could be set by the commission at levels that will assure that a significant portion of the gains realized by above standard performance will be passed as benefits to consumers (e.g., in terms of lower rate increases than those that would have been called for in the absence of above standard performance). Only a portion of those gains would be retained by the firm. As is now the case, the regulator, of course, can continue to monitor quality of service and provide appropriate incentives to maintain or improve quality and reliability. It is usually possible to improve productivity performance at the expense of service standards and the continued monitoring of service quality should serve to attenuate this type of strategic behavior.

Pricing Efficiency

The lack of incentives for efficient pricing of services in the framework of conventional rate-of-return regulation, has been extensively discussed in the literature (see Baron (1980a, 1980b) and Sherman (1977, 1980) among others). In addressing this problem Chaudry and Sudit (1982) note that while CIPRAC yields an overall percentage rate adjustment, it is not intended as a prescription for a uniform rate change for all services. In the framework of CIPRAC, Chaudry and Sudit (1982) propose that the regulated company should be given freedom to set rates for specific services in an efficient manner so long as the weighted sum of the rates increases does not exceed the percent change, $[\Sigma_{j=1}^{m}(\dot{P}_j/P_j)\beta_j]^A$, allowed by the adjustment formulae in (8.6). While the practice does not necessarily guarantee equilibrium at Ramsey efficient prices, the built-in productivity incentives in (8.6) are likely to motivate movement toward elasticity-oriented and more efficient pricing.

One way to improve actual TFP performance is to set the rates for specific services to be inversely related to their respective price elasticities of demand. The lower the relative elasticity, the higher the relative price of one service with respect to another. This type of pricing, if pursued, will increase the rate of growth in total output and productivity generated by a given rate of growth in total inputs. The resulting improvement in actual TFP performance will, via the interim adjustment formulae in (8.6) and (8.6a), benefit the company by increasing its earnings. Hence, the combined effect of built-in productivity and profit incentives is likely, other things being equal, to motivate movement in the direction of welfare efficient pricing. These price changes could, of course, be made subject to Commission review within a specified period. This will ensure that the Commission is still retaining a measure of control over specific prices.

A Retrospective Illustration of the Effects of Productivity Based Regulation

Sudit (1979, pp. 67–68) provided a retrospective empirical analysis designed to assess the potential effects of implementing productivity based rate adjustment clause. The rate adjustment formula that was tested is an earlier version of CIPRAC without built-in rate of return incentives. Specifically, the tested adjustment clause was the one defined in (8.6) and (8.6a) with $\delta = 0$ and $\mu = 0$. The retrospective test described below was designed to examine how this rate adjustment clause would have worked had it been implemented in five regulated industries.

Five regulated industries, with the two major public utility sectors among them, were selected. Total factor productivity estimates based on Laspeyres indexes for these industries were available for the 1948–1966 period. Those productivity growth rates are presented in table 8-3 (column one). Rough estimates of changes in weighted input costs (labor and capital) associated with the chosen industries were computed for the corresponding periods based on national income statistics. This was done by making rough estimates of average capital, labor, and materials shares in total cost over the period and applying these shares as weights to changes in overall labor, capital, and materials costs in the manufacturing sector. The formula in (8.6) was applied to the rates of growth in productivity and unit input costs to

Table 8-3. Automatic Rate Adjustments versus Actual Price Changes, 1948-1966 (estimates of average annual percentage)

Industry	*Total Factor Productivity Growth*	*Hypothetical Change in Rates (Formula)*	*Change in Rates (Actual)*
Air transportation	8.0	−2.0	−0.3
Railroad and related services	5.0	0	+1.0
Electric and gas utilities	4.0	0	+1.1
Telephone and Telegraph	4.0	0	+1.8
Intercity bus lines	2.0	+4.0	+3.5

Source: Sudit (1979) p. 67.

Table 8-4. Automatic Rate Adjustments versus Actual Price Changes, 1966-1976 (estimates of average annual percentage)

Industry	*Total Factor Productivity Growth*	*Hypothetical Change in Rates (Formula)*	*Change in Rates (Actual)*
Air transportation	4.0	+7.0	+6.6
Railroad and related services	3.0	+7.0	+5.8
Electric and gas utilities	3.0	+6.0	+8.8
Telephone and Telegraph	3.0	+5.0	+3.0
Intercity bus lines	1.0	+9.0	+9.2

Source: Sudit (1979) p. 69.

compute the automatic rate change required by the adjustment technique. These formula-required rate changes are presented in column two of table 8.3. They reflect the changes in rates that hypothetically would have occurred had the adjustment formula in (8.6) been applied throughout the period. Finally, the formula based rate adjustments are compared (in column three) with approximate estimates of the actual rate changes (as reflected in available price indexes for the respective industries) that did in fact take place during the period.

The estimates in the table suggest that if automatic rate adjustment had been implemented, they would have either fallen short of or stayed relatively close to commission approved rate increases. Although these numbers represent rough approximations of national averages, they could be interpreted as suggestive of the efficiency potential inherent in appropriate automatic adjustment clauses. The findings in table 8-3 provide at least tentative empirical support to theoretical expectations that automatic rate adjustments are likely to reduce the frequency of hearings and the magnitude of regulatory lags. Also, the numbers suggest that public concerns to the effect that automatic adjustment could result in excessive growth in rates and profits of regulated firms may be too great.

Table 8-4 presents the same analysis for the 1966–1976 period, with the estimates generally compiled in a way similar to the computations for table 8-3. Since total factor productivity estimates for the period were not available at the time of the original study, reductions in productivity growth proportional to the reduction in national productivity performance relative to the previous decade were imputed. Also, the dramatic fuel price increases of the 1970's were taken into account in computing roughly estimated overall growth rates in weighted input prices. For all industries, except for telephone and telegraph, formula adjustments fell short of actual commission approved rate increases.

The comparisons in the two tables may provide some conjectural insights as to the efficiency of regulations. They seem to indicate that commissions, on the average, have shown propensities to approve higher rates than may be justified by cost and productivity changes. In so doing, they have generally resorted to more cumbersome and costly procedures to accomplish a task that could have been attained more efficiently by more frequent resort to automatic corrections. Finally, the reader should bear in mind that the hypothetical rate changes in table 8-3 and 8-4 probably overstate the rate increases that would have been obtained by the adjustment clause. Since it was impossible to estimate retrospectively any effects of the built-in incentive in terms of improved productivity and cost performance, it stands to reason that the price effects of the adjustment clauses would have been even more favorable.

Productivity Based Pricing in the Public Sector

As observed in the first section of this chapter, some services are sold by the government to recipients in the marketplace (i.e., postal services). In most countries with mixed economies, governments periodically choose to nationalize whole industries or individual companies and sell their products. In socialist and communist countries most private goods are sold by the public sector. For services sold by governments or government owned enterprises the use of modified versions of the productivity based formula outlined in equation (8.6) to price those goods and services may be appropriate and even desirable. Public sector enterprises can show surpluses or deficits, not profits or losses. Consequently, the rate of return constraints in (8.6a) do not apply. Instead, budget constraints and deficit constraints may be appropriate. For example, governments may put an upper limit to funds they wish to allocate to specific enterprises to finance operating or capital budget expenditures. Alternatively, they may authorize nationalized companies to raise funds in capital markets within certain prescribed limits. Any such constraints may be added to the pricing formula in (8.6), which in itself remains an appropriate framework for productivity based pricing in the public sector.

A major advantage of applying equation (8.6) to pricing in the public sector is the introduction of built-in productivity incentives and cost efficiency incentives, as described in preceeding sections of this chapter. If management and employees of public enterprises are permitted to keep a portion of the surpluses in the form of productivity and efficiency bonuses, they are likely to be motivated to improve productivity performance and economize on purchases by exceeding prespecified total factor productivity and outperforming input price standards. Recipients of goods and services will benefit as portions of the incentive induced productivity and cost efficiency gains are passed on in the form of price decreases or lower price increases. In the process, the costs of government audits and controls can be reduced.

Crew et al. (1979) examined several alternative productivity based pricing mechanisms for nationalized industries in the United Kingdom. According to one of their proposed schemes, nationalized companies would keep half of the surplus funds generated by above target productivity performance, thereby providing built-in productivity incentives. Economy incentives were guaranteed by adherence to market referenced increases in input prices. Actual practices for pricing goods and services provided by the British public sector contain no built-in productivity or purchasing incentives. The same is true for pricing practices in the public sectors of most countries including the U.S. Hence, the opportunities for improving operational efficiencies in public sector enterprises by resorting to productivity based management in general and productivity based pricing in particular should not be overlooked.

Notes

1. See Charnes A., Cooper W.W. and Rhodes E., "Measuring the Efficiency of Decision Making Units." *European Journal of Operations Research 2* (1978) pp. 429–444.
2. The superscript 2 in (8.1a) and (8.1b) denotes variables and weights of DMU number 2. None of these variables and weights is raised to the second power.
3. Program I is Program Follow Through (PFT) and Program II is Non-Follow Through (NFT), discussed in the following section, pp. 127–132.

In figure 8-2, Program I is denoted by PFT and Program II is denoted by NFT. Envelope I is the PFT-α-envelope in figure 8-2, and Envelope II is the NFT-α-envelope.

REFERENCES

Abramowitz, M., 1956, "Resources and Output Trends in the U.S. since 1870," *American Economic Review* 46, no. 2:5–23.

Arzac, E.R. and F.R. Edwards, 1979, "Efficiency in Regulated and Unregulated Firms: An Iconoclastic View of the Averch-Johnson Thesis," in M. Crew, Ed., *Problems in Public Utility Economics and Regulation*, Lexington Books.

Backman, J. and Kirsten, J.B., 1974, "Comprehensive Adjustment Clause for Telephone Companies," *Public Utilities Fortnightly*, November, 28:21–26.

Baron, D.P., 1980a, "Regulatory Strategies Under Asymmetric Information," Working Paper, Northwestern University, Evanston, Illinois.

Baumol, W.J. 1970, "Reasonable Rules for Rate Regulation: Plausible Policies for an Imperfect World" in P.W. MacAvoy Ed., *The Crisis of the Regulatory Commissions*, W.W. Norton, New York.

Beckman, M.J. and R. Sato, 1969, "Aggregate Production Functions and Types of Technical Change," *American Economic Review* 59:88–101.

Branson, S., 1975, "Monetarist and Keynesian Models of the Transmission of Inflation," *American Economic Review*, 65:115–119, May 1975.

Brendt, E.R., and Mohammed S. Khaled, 1979, "Parametric Productivity Measurement and Choice among Flexible Functional Forms," *Journal of Political Economy*, December 87:1220–1245.

Bruno, M., 1978, "Duality, Intermediate Inputs and Value-Added," in Fuss and

McFadden, Eds., *Production Economics: A Dual Approach to Theory and Applications*, North-Holland.

Bureau of Labor Statistics, 1983, *Multifactor Productivity Indexes*, U.S. Department of Labor, 83–153, April.

Charnes, A. and W.W. Cooper, and E. Rhodes, 1978, "Measuring the Efficiency of Decision Making Units," *European Journal of Operational Research* 2:429–444.

Charnes, A., and W.W. Cooper, 1980, "Management Science Relations for Evaluation and Management Accountability," *Journal of Enterprise Management*, 2:143–162.

Charnes, A. and W.W. Cooper, 1973, "An Explicit General Solution in Linear Fractional Programming," *Naval Research Logistics Quarterly*, 20(3).

Chaudry, M.A. and E.F. Sudit, 1984, "Alternatives for Productivity-Based Pricing in Public Utility Regulation—The Case of Telecommunications" (unpublished paper).

Christensen, L. and D.W. Jorgenson, 1970, "U.S. Real Product and Real Factor Input, 1929–67," *Review of Income and Wealth* 16, No. 1:19–50.

Christensen, L., and D.W. Jorgenson, and L.J. Lau, 1971, "Conjugate Duality and the Transcendental Logarithmic Function," Econometrica 39:255–256.

Christensen, L., and D.W. Jorgenson, L.J. Lau, 1973, "Transcendental Logarithmic Production Frontiers," *Review of Economics and Statistics* 55, No. 1:28–45.

Cohen, B.I., 1972, "Foreign Investment by U.S. Corporations As a Way of Reducing Risk," *Yale University Economic Growth Center*, Paper No. 151, September 1972.

Crandall, R.W., 1981, *The U.S. Steel Industry in Recurrent Crisis: Policy Options in a Competitive World,* Brookings Institution, March 1981.

Crew, M.A., P. R. Kleindorfer, and E.F. Sudit, 1979, "Incentives for Efficiency in the Nationalized Industries: Beyond the 1978 White Paper," *Journal of Industrial Affairs* 7, No. 1:11–15.

Crew, M.A., Ed., 1979, *Problems in Public Utility Economics and Regulation*, Lexington, Massachusetts: Lexington Books.

Denny, M., M. Fuss, and L. Waverman, 1981, "The Measurement and Interpretation of Total Factor Productivity in Related Industries, with an Application of Canadian Telecommunications," in T.G. Cowing and R.E. Stevenson, Eds. *Productivity Measurement in Regulated Industries*, New York: Academic Press.

Denison, E.F., 1974, *Accounting for United States Economic Growth, 1929–1969*, Washington, D.C.: Brookings.

Diewert, E.W., 1971, "An Application of the Shephard Duality Theorem: A Generalized Leontief Production Function," *Journal of Political Economy* 79, no. 3:481–507.

Diewert, E.W., 1976, "Exact and Superlative Index Numbers," *Journal of Econometrics* 4, no. 2:115–46.

Diewert E.W. 1978, "Hicks' Aggregation Theorem and the Existence of a real Value-Added Function" in M. Fuss and D. McFadden Eds. *Production Eco-*

nomics: A Dual Approach to Theory and Applications, Vol. 2. North Holland Publishing Company, Amsterdam.

Divisia, F., 1926, *L'indice monetaire et la theorie de la monnaie,* Sirey, Paris: Societé Anonyme du Recueil.

Edwards, F.R. 1977, "Managerial Objectives in Regulated Industries: Expense-Preference Behavior in Banking," *Journal of Political Economy*, 85:147–162.

Eldor, D., C.H. Shami, and E.F. Sudit, 1979, "Production-Cost Elasticities in Product and Factor Markets," *Journal of Economics and Business* 31, 84–89.

Eldor, D., and E.F. Sudit, 1981, "Productivity-Based Net Income Analysis," *OMEGA—The International Journal of Management Science*, 9, No. 6:605–611.

Eldor, D., and E.F. Sudit, 1982, "Alternative Specifications of Returns to Scale and Joint Estimation of Factor Demand and Production Functions in Telecommunications," *Review of Business and Economic Research*, 18 No. 1:15–26 Fall 1982.

Fabricant, S., 1942, *Employment in Manufacturing, 1899–1939*, New York, National Bureau for Economic Research.

Farrel, M.J., 1957, "The Measurement of Productive Efficiency," *Journal of the Royal Statistical Society*, Series A, 3:253–190.

Fishelson, G., 1977, "Telecommunications: CES Production Function," *Applied Economics* 9, No. 1:9–18.

Fisher, I., 1922, *The Making of Index Numbers*, Boston: Houghton Mifflin.

Friedlaender, A.F., C. Winston and K. Wang, 1983, "Costs, Technology and Productivity in the U.S. Automobile Industry," *The Bell Journal of Economics*, 14, No. 1:1–20.

Hartman, R. 1976, "Factor Demand with Output Price Uncertainty", *American Economic Review*, 66, 675–81.

Hasenkamp, G., 1976, *Specification and Estimation of Multiple Output Production Functions*, Berlin: Springer Verlag.

Hicks, J.R., 1946, *Value and Capital*, 2nd edition, Oxford: Clarendon Press.

Hughes, J.S., D.E. Logue, and R.J. Sweeney, 1975, "Corporate International Diversification and Market Assigned Measures of Risk and Diversification," *Journal of Financial and Quantitative Analysis*, November.

Hulten, C.R., 1973, "Divisia Index Numbers," *Econometrica* 41:1017–26.

Hulten, C.R., 1975, "Technical Change and the Reproducibility of Capital," *American Economic Review* 65:956–965.

Hulten, C.R., 1979, "On the Importance of Productivity Change," *American Economic Review*, 6:126–136.

Hulten, C.R., and M. Nishimizu, 1980, "The Importance of Productivity Change in the Economic Growth of Nine Industrialized Countries," in Eds. S. Meital and N.M. Meltz, *Lagging Productivity Growth: Causes and Remedies* Cambridge, Massachusetts: Ballinger Publishing Company.

Ijiri, Y., and H. Itami, 1973, "Quadratic Cost Volume Relationship and Timing of Demand Information," *The Accounting Review*, 48(4):766–782.

Ishikawa, A., and E.F. Sudit, 1981, "Selective Sequential Zero Base Budgeting Procedures Based on Total Factor Productivity Indicators," *Management Science*, 27, No. 5:534–546 May 1981.

Itami, H., 1977, *Adaptive Behavior: Management Control and Information Analysis*, Studies in Accounting Research No. 15, American Accounting Association.

Ivanyi, T., 1976, "Investigation of the Dynamics and the Efficiency of Primary Production Factors with the Aid of an Unchanged Inverse Matrix," in *Input-Output Techniques*, Akademiai-Kiado, Budapest.

Jagpal, H.S., and E.F. Sudit 1978, "Economic Efficiency Measures in Retentive and Expansive Marketing of Financial Services," *Industrial Marketing Management*, 7, 423–430 December 1978.

Jagpal, H.S., and E.F. Sudit, 1979, "Theory and Measurement of Joint Marketing Mix Effects and Interactions in Multiproduct Firms," *Proceedings of the American Marketing Association*, August 1979.

Jagpal, H.S., and E.F. Sudit, and H.D. Vinod, 1979, "The Measurement of Advertising Interactions in Sales Response Functions," *Journal of Advertising Research*, 19, No. 3:41–48. June 1979.

Jagpal, H.S. and E.F. Sudit, and H.D. Vinod, 1982, "Marketing Mix Interactions Using Translog Functions," *Journal of Business*, 55, No. 3:401–415. June 1982.

Jorgenson, D.W., and Z. Griliches, 1967, "The Explanation of Productivity Change," *Review of Economic Studies* 34, No. 99, 249–83.

Jorgenson, D.W., and Z. Griliches, 1972, "Issues in Growth Accounting: A Reply to Edward F. Denison," *Survey of Current Business* 52, No. 5, Part 2; 65–94.

Kendrick, J.W., 1961, *Productivity Trends in the U.S.*, New York, National Bureau of Economic Research.

Kendrick, J.W., 1973, *Postwar Productivity Trends in the U.S. 1948–69,* New York, National Bureau for Economic Research.

Kendrick, J.W., 1973, *Postwar Productivity Trends in the U.S.,* 1948–69, New York, National Bureau of Economic Research.

Kendrick, J.W., 1975, "Efficiency Incentives and Cost Factors in Public Utility Automatic Revenue Adjustment Clauses," *Bell Journal of Economics* 6:392–415.

Kendrick, J.W., 1977, *Understanding Productivity*, John Hopkins University Press.

Kendrick, J.W., and E. Grossman, 1980, *Trends and Cycles in Productivity in the United States*, Baltimore: John Hopkins University Press.

Kendrick, J.W., 1980, "Productivity Trends in the U.S.," in Eds. Maital S., and Meltz, N.M., *Lagging Productivity Growth: Causes and Remedies*, Ballinger Publishing Company, Cambridge, Massachusetts.

Kenen, P.B., 1978, "New Views of Exchange Rates and Old View of Policy," *American Economic Review*, 68, No. 2:398–405.

Khaled, M.S., 1978, "Productivity Analysis and Functional Specification: A

Parametric Approach," Ph.D. Dissertation, University of British Columbia, Department of Economics, April 1978.

Kravis, I.B., 1976, "A Survey of International Comparisons of Productivity, *Economic Journal*, 86:1–44. March 1976.

Latimer, M.A., 1974, "The Cost and Efficiency Revenue Adjustment Clause," *Public Utility Fortnightly*, (August):19–24.

Leibenstein, H., 1966, "Allocative vs. X-Efficiency," *American Economic Review*, 56:392–415.

Levich, R.M., 1982, "How the Rise of the Dollar Took Forecasters by Surprise," *Euromoney*, August 1982, 98–112.

Levich, R.M., 1982, "How to Compare Chance with Forecasting Expertise," *Euromoney*, August 1981, 61–79.

Lindbeck, A., 1981, "Industrial Policy as an Issue in the Economic Environment," *The World Economy*, 4, No. 4:391–406. December 1981.

Lindsay, W.W., 1977, "Automatic Adjustment Clauses as a Means for Improving Regulation," in J.L. O'Donnell, Ed., *Adapting Regulation to Shortages, Curtailment and Inflation*, Michigan State University Press, 1977.

Malinvaud, E., 1953, "Capital Accumulation and Efficient Allocation of Resources," *Econometrica* 21, 2:233–68.

Nadiri, I.M., 1970, "Some Approaches to the Theory and Measurement of Total Factor Productivity: A Survey," *Journal of Economic Literature* 8:1137–77.

Nadiri, I.M., and M.A. Schankerman, 1981, "The Structure of Production, Technological Change, and the Rate of Growth of Total Factor Productivity in the U.S. Bell System," in Eds. Cowing, T.G. and Stevenson, R.E., *Productivity Measurement in Regulated Industries*, New York: Academic Press.

Nerlov, Mark, 1963, "Returns to Scale in Electricity Supply," in Eds. C.F. Christ et al. *Measurement in Economics: Studies in Mathematical Economics and Econometrics in Memory of Yehuda Grunfeld*, Stanford, California: Stanford University Press.

Nichols, E., 1955, *Ruling Principles of Utility Regulation, Rate of Return,* Washington: Public Utility Reports.

Nyitrai, V., 1976, "The Role of Input-Output Tables in Analyzing Industrial Efficiency," in *Input-Output Techniques,* Akademiai Kiado, Budapest.

Pasinetti, Luigi L., 1977, *Lectures on the Theory of Production*, New York: Columbia University Press.

Pugel, T.A., Y. Kimuara, and R.G. Hawkins, 1983, "Semiconductors and Computers: Emerging Competitive Battlegrounds in the Asia-Pacific Region," in R.M. Moxon, T.W. Roehl and J.F. Truitt, Eds., *International Business Strategies in the Asia-Pacific Region*, Vol. 2, Industry Studies, Greenwich, Connecticut: JAI Press.

Ravid, A.S., and E.F. Sudit, 1983, "Determination of Profit Maximizing Quantitative Standards for a Competitive Risk-Neutral Firm Under Price Uncertainty," unpublished paper, Graduate School of Management, Rutgers University, Newark, New Jersey.

Reid, S.D., 1981, "The Decision Maker and Export Entry and Expansion," *Journal of International Business Research*, 12 (fall 1981) No. 2:101–112.

Renshaw, E.F. 1978, "A Note on Cost and Efficiency Revenue Adjustment Clauses," *Public Utilities Fortnightly*, January 5, 37–78.

Robichek, A.A., 1978, "Regulation and Modern Finance Theory," *Journal of Finance*, 33, 693–705.

Robinson, Joan, 1969, *The Accumulation of Capital*, 3rd edition, London, Macmillan.

Rugman, A., 1976, "Risk Reduction by International Diversification," *Journal of International Business Studies*, 7, No. 2:75–80.

Rugman, A., 1979, *International Diversification of the Multinational Enterprise*, Lexington Books, Lexington, Massachusetts.

Rugman, A., 1980, *Multinationals in Canada, Performance and Economic Impact*, Martinus Nijhoff Publishing 1980.

Rymes, T.K., 1971, *On Concepts of Capital and Technical Change*, Cambridge: Cambridge University Press.

Schmidt, M. 1980, *Automatic Adjustment Clauses: Theory and Application*, MSU Public Utility Studies, Michigan State University Press.

Scott, F.A., 1980, "Fuel Adjustment Clauses and Profit Risk," in M. Crew, Ed., *Issues in Public Utility Pricing Regulation*, Lexington Books.

Severn, A., 1974, "Investor Evaluation of Foreign and Domestic Risk," *Journal of Finance*, (May): 545–550.

Shakun, M.F. 1981, "Formalizing Conflict Resolution in Policy making", *International Journal of General Systems*, 7, No. 3.

Shakun, M.F. 1981, "Policy Making and Meaning as Design of Purposeful Systems," *International Journal of General Systems*, 7, No. 3.

Shakun, M. and E.F. Sudit, 1983, "Effectiveness, Productivity and Design of Purposeful Systems, *International Journal of General Systems*, 9, 205–215.

Shephard, R.W., 1970, *Theory on Cost and Production Functions*, Princeton, New Jersey: Princeton University Press.

Sherman, R., 1977, "Financial Aspects of the Regulated Firm," *Southern Economic Journal*, 44 (October):240–248.

Sherman, R., 1980, "Hope Against Hope," in M. Crew, Ed., *Issues in Public Utility Pricing and Regulation*, Lexington Massachusetts Lexington Books.

Solow, Robert M. 1957, "Technical Change and the Aggregate Production Function," *Review of Economics and Statistics*, 29, 312–20.

Sinden, F. 1980, "Inflation Adjustment Formulas and Efficiency Incentives," a paper presented at the Twelfth Annual Conference of the institute of Public Utilities, Williamsburg, Virginia, Dec. 1–3, 1980.

Sraffa, P., 1960, *Production of Commodities by Means of Commodities*, Cambridge University Press, London.

Star, S., 1974, "Accounting for the Growth of Output," *American Economic Review* 64, No. 1:123–35.

Stern, A., 1979, "The Impact of World Price Changes Under Alternative Exchange Rates," *Journal of Economics and Business*, 32 No. 1:79–85 Fall 1979.

Sudit, E.F., 1979 "Automatic Rate Adjustment Based on Total Factor Productivity Performance in Public Utility Regulation," in M. Crew, Ed., (1979).

Sudit, E.F., 1984, "The Role of Comparative Productivity Accounting in Export Decisions," *Journal of International Business Studies* (forthcoming).

Theil, H., 1968, "On the Geometry of the Numerical Approximation of Cost of Living and Real Income Indices," *De Economist* 116.

Törnqvist, L., 1936, "The Bank of Finland's Consumption Price Index," *Bank of Finland Monthly Bulletin* 10, 1–8.

Törnqvist, L., 1936, "The Bank of Finland's Consumption Price Index," *Bank of Finland Monthly Bulletin*, 10, 1–8.

Tsurumi, H., and Y. Tsurami, 1980, "A Beysian Test of the Product Life Cycle Hypothesis as Applied to the U.S. Demand for Color T.V. Sets," *International Economic Review*, 21, 3:23–35 October 1980.

Vinod, H.D., 1968, "Econometrics of Joint Production," *Econometrica* 36: 322–36.

Vinod, H.D., Ridge Estimation of a Translog Production Function," Business and Economics Statistics Section Proceeding, St. Louis, Missouri: American Statistical Association.

Vinod, H.D., 1976, "Cononical Ridge and Econometrics of Joint Production," *Journal of Econometrics*, 4, 147–66.

Vinod, H.D., 1978, "A Survey of Ridge Regression and Related techniques for Improvement over Ordinary Least Squares," *Review of Economic and Statistics,* 60, No. 1:121–131.

Vogelsang I. and Y. Finsinger, 1979, "A Regulatory Adjustment Process for Optimal Pricing by Multiproduct Monopoly Firms." *The Bell Journal of Economics* 10, No. 1:157–171.

NAME INDEX

SUBJECT INDEX

GPSR Compliance

The European Union's (EU) General Product Safety Regulation (GPSR) is a set of rules that requires consumer products to be safe and our obligations to ensure this.

If you have any concerns about our products, you can contact us on ProductSafety@springernature.com

In case Publisher is established outside the EU, the EU authorized representative is:

Springer Nature Customer Service Center GmbH
Europaplatz 3
69115 Heidelberg, Germany

Batch number: 10830943

Printed by Printforce, the Netherlands